THE
25 HABITS
OF
HIGHLY
SUCCESSFUL
INVESTORS

How to Invest for Profit in Today's Changing Markets

PETER SANDER

Aadamsmedia
AVON, MASSACHUSETTS

Published by
Adams Media, a division of F+W Media, Inc.
57 Littlefield Street, Avon, MA 02322. U.S.A.
www.adamsmedia.com

ISBN 10: 1-4405-5662-8
ISBN 13: 978-1-4405-5662-3
eISBN 10: 1-4405-5663-6
eISBN 13: 978-1-4405-5663-0

Printed in the United States of America.

10   9   8   7   6   5   4

Library of Congress Cataloging-in-Publication Data
Sander, Peter J.
   The 25 habits of highly successful investors / Peter Sander.
      p. cm.
   ISBN-13: 978-1-4405-5662-3 (pbk.)
   ISBN-10: 1-4405-5662-8 (pbk.)
   ISBN-13: 978-1-4405-5663-0 (ebook)
   ISBN-10: 1-4405-5663-6 (ebook)
   1. Investments. 2. Portfolio management. I. Title. II. Title: Twenty five habits of
highly successful investors.
   HG4521.S33167 2012
   332.6–dc23
                              2012030650

This book is available at quantity discounts for bulk purchases.
For information, please call 1-800-289-0963.

DEDICATION

The 25 Habits of Highly Successful Investors is dedicated to you active investors who have the sense of purpose and independence of thought to make your own investing decisions, and who seek a novel and creative but yet proven and somewhat structured approach to making those decisions. With *25 Habits*, you'll gain a thought process, and you will at least learn to ask the right questions even if you choose not to manage your own investments. If nothing else, these habits are a smart place to start to appraise any business—including the one you work for.

ACKNOWLEDGMENTS

I would like to recognize my editor, Peter Archer, for coming up with the *25 Habits* concept, and motivating me to assemble my forty-five years of investing experience into this useful and readable construct. In addition, no book happens without the added value of exercise to keep a body in shape and a mind clear, and to that end I offer my ongoing thanks to my exercise companions. And of course, as with all of my books, my boys Julian and Jonathan and new fiancée Marjorie get credit for the inspiration and support to keep writing.

Contents

or losing it? Are you competing on price alone or on some other value add? Is the company positioned for success?

Put on Your Street Shoes: *As you think like a marketer, also think like a marketee—a customer. How is the company perceived by the customer? Look around at its facilities, online presence, etc. Does the experience "click"? Could it be improved?*

Sense the Management Style: *Are managers achievement oriented and all-in for the shareholders, or are they power oriented and all-in for themselves?*

Look for Signs of Value, Signs of Unvalue: *Assess each company for its ten signs of value and unvalue as per the list.*

Do Your Threes—Three Pros, Three Cons: *When you have your facts and impressions together, list the three strongest reasons to buy the investment and the three strongest to avoid it.*

Buy with a Margin of Safety: *Once you've decided that a company is good to own, now (and only now) decide if the price is right. Give yourself a margin of safety in case you're wrong.*

Buy Smart—When You Decide to Buy: *Watch price behavior before you buy to try to find a good entry point, but don't shirk a good entry point just to save a few cents.*

INTRODUCTION

Investing Can Be Habit Forming

"Motivation is what gets you started.
Habit is what keeps you going."

—Jim Ryun, former world record holder, one mile run

You have some money to invest. Now what?

Maybe you've been investing actively for years, but you're not that happy with your results. Up one year, way down the next, then sideways in a third year while the markets marched steadily upward.

Isn't it a little like golf or some other precision sport? You play a really good round one day, really bad the next, and a few good holes in an otherwise pretty dreary round the following week. Or cooking. You do a really awesome puffy pancake one Sunday morning; then the next Sunday it does a face plant on the bottom of the pan and you burn it. On the third Sunday it's okay, but the kids aren't smiling about it anymore.

Sheer instinct in any of these situations makes you want to climb back into the saddle. As in golf or cooking, you would like to improve your investing techniques and intuition. You would like to keep doing it yourself—mostly yourself, anyway. You want to get to the point where you can do it (1) well; (2) with some consistency; and (3) without blowing your mind trying to remember what you did the last time.

Like these other skill-based activities, you approach your investing to (1) achieve or exceed your expectations; (2) be consistent and reliable; and (3) do it without beating your brains out or spending hours of precious personal time on it.

You can argue that good investing is a matter of skill, experience, foresight, time, energy, and a fair dose of luck. All of the above are involved in golf and cooking, and I would submit that they're all involved in investing. But, especially in today's world (for most of us, anyway) of other priorities, where we can't—or don't want to—spend the day in front of the computer checking and analyzing investments, good investing requires good *habits*.

Without good habits, you may find yourself stuck in a pattern of lackluster, inconsistent investing performance. With good habits, you'll be right more of the time (notice I didn't say *all* the time). You'll feel better and sleep better because you did the right things. And you'll take less time—or *spend more productive time*—to do it.

In that spirit, I offer you *The 25 Habits of Highly Successful Investors*.

What Do I Mean by "Habit?"

When you think of the word "habits," what comes first to mind? For most of us, especially prior to the advent of Stephen Covey's 1989 blockbuster, *The Seven Habits of Highly Effective People*, the word *habit* probably conjured up the notion of *bad* habits such as smoking, drinking, cracking your knuckles, or tapping on the dinner table with your fingernails. Habits that are bad for you, annoy others, or some combination of the two. Not a helpful concept for an investing book, right?

The 25 Habits of Highly Successful Investors isn't about kicking bad investing habits. It isn't necessarily about turning the things you do already into habits, although I'm hopeful that you've been doing at least some of these things right already.

It's really about structuring some of the things you do and have experienced, together with some elements of investing that you probably *don't* do and haven't experienced, into a "smart" of repeatable exercises that ultimately improve your investing performance. If all goes well, *25 Habits* will improve your performance while taking less of your time (or at least investing more of it wisely) and making you more comfortable with the whole investing process.

Straight Out of the Dictionary

I have a habit of using dictionary definitions to highlight terms in titles or concepts I want to discuss. Accordingly, here's the dictionary definition for *habit* from the *Free Dictionary* by Farlex:

A *habit* is:

a. A recurrent, often unconscious pattern of behavior that is acquired through frequent repetition.

b. An established disposition of the mind or character.

As an investor, particularly a time-constrained investor, which most of us are, you should establish a routine. Instead of approaching each investment decision as if you've never made one before, you want a proven method that works for *you.* You want a method that is repeatable. You want a method that is a process, but is a process simple and clear enough to follow without spending undue time thinking about it. You want to concentrate on the *result*, and that result is guided by what becomes "a pattern of behavior," an "established disposition of the mind or character"—something repeatable over and over without thinking about it too much.

Where Do These Habits Come From?

*"The chains of habit are generally too small
to be felt until they are too strong to be broken."*

—Samuel Johnson, British author and lexicographer

This book is dedicated to setting forth twenty-five "chains of habit" I believe make sense for today's informed, long-term, goal-oriented, individual investor. I have culled from my own forty-four years of personal investing experience and the experience of other icons of a habitual, *value-oriented* investing style, namely Warren Buffett, Peter Lynch, Benjamin Graham, and other followers of that investing "school."

Once again, I have thrown in some terms. *Long-term, goal-oriented, individual investor, value-oriented investing style.* Before going further, we should take a short side trip into what I mean by each of these terms:

Long Term

You hear the term all the time—yet—what really is the long term for an investor? We hear a lot about "buy and hold," and many of us at one time or another have done it. (Or our parents did. Mine bought thirty-five shares of General Motors and stuffed the certificate in a safe deposit box. From that time forward they bought only GM cars. They apparently intended to hold the stock forever.) That was in an era where change came more slowly and industries lasted longer—think about railroads, radio, the auto industry—significant change took thirty, fifty, even 100 years to occur. Today, industries change much more rapidly. Think about plays in the Internet, PC, restaurant, or entertainment businesses for just a few examples of industries that change rapidly or even run their course in five, ten, or twenty years. Indeed, even stalwart Microsoft has defended against its antitrust suitors on account of its fears about survival, not against competitors, but against technological evolution and eventual demise of the PC. So what is long term? For any given investment—maybe five to seven years, depending on the industry.

Goal Oriented

This sounds a bit fluffy, but what is your investing goal? Fast, short-term cash? Longer-term growth? To hit an eventual number for college education, retirement, or simple financial security? The approach in *25 Habits* has a foot in both camps—to achieve long-term, relatively risk-averse growth, with a modest amount of cash return thrown in during the meantime to enhance your total return and "pay yourself now." Another goal: to achieve a *modestly* better return—a few percentage points better than the overall market return with lots of singles, doubles, and base runners, not so many home runs and strikeouts.

Individual

25 Habits is aimed at the individual investor, that is, the investor who takes charge of his or her own investments. Such investors may do all of their own investing, or may throw some or all of their investing decisions "over the wall" to a professional adviser or fund manager (mutual funds) or index creator (ETFs, or Exchange-Traded Funds) to balance their decision making and lighten the load for at least part of the portfolio. The individual investor making his or her own decisions follows habits, while the investor working with or through the adviser looks for evidence that a professional adviser is "on board" with some of the more important ones. Incidentally, Habit 9: Appraise Funds Realistically, is about making sure a fund is worthwhile and is in sync with your investing objectives.

Investor

You're not a trader, not a speculator, not someone climbing on board with the latest investing "story" like Facebook or Webvan years ago; you're not someone looking for something to brag about at the next cocktail party. *25 Habits* investors look for solid longer-term returns on their precious capital deployed rationally in good businesses, and they invest in shares of businesses as if they'd like to own the whole thing.

Value Oriented

This book follows the so-called *value* school of investing. "Value" investing takes a rational view of the financial and intangible fundamentals of a business and values that business simply in terms of what cash return you will net from it over the course of ownership—nothing more or nothing less. When you invest, you look at that "intrinsic" value against the *price* of the business—the share price. If it looks like a bargain, *that is*, if the price gives you a margin of safety, you buy it.

As suggested above, *25 Habits* is drawn from my own investing experience but is heavily influenced by the icons of value investing, especially Warren Buffett. The Buffettonian style, which considers the growth potential to be an important component of value, is my primary inspiration—which, incidentally, dismisses the notion held by many mutual funds and their followers that a fund must be categorized either as growth *or* value.

Former Fidelity Magellan fund manager Peter Lynch gives us the notion in his *One Up on Wall Street* and elsewhere that the best businesses are the ones that look good "on the street," that is, on Main Street. The basic question is, are they succeeding in the marketplace? If they are, then they will succeed in the *stock* market eventually as well.

This and my own personal experience drive home the notion that future *financial* performance is at least as much a function of future *marketplace* performance and other "strategic intangibles" and less a function of *past* financial performance. It's this latter element that most investment analysts center on. As an investor, you're really more interested in future results than past results. Thus, several of the *25 Habits* are aimed at intangibles—Habits 13–15, Put on Your Marketing Hat, Put on Your Street Shoes, and Sense the Management Style. They offer tips aimed at assessing future performance.

To Whom Do I Speak?

With these ideas in place, what do I assume about you, your experience, and your base of knowledge?

1. *You're busy.* This isn't what you do for a living. You have a "day job" or a retirement base, and you want to grow what you have or earn, but you probably have only a few hours a week, at most, to dedicate to your investments.
2. *You're an investor.* Not a trader, not a speculator, and not a market player. (There are lots of other books out there for that.) You're investing for moderate longer-term return on your money.
3. *You're a* stock *investor.* Most of what I talk about involves the purchase and ownership of stocks, not bonds, gold, other commodities, real estate, money market instruments, and other investments. Although some principles, like Habits 23–24, Don't Marry Your Investments and Sell When There's Something Better to Buy, do apply.
4. *You've done this before.* In *25 Habits*, I don't explain what the stock market is or how it works, how online brokers work, or how mutual funds and other types of investments work. The basis for this book is owning common

stocks—shares of businesses you would like to own as a business.

5. *You want to do at least some of this yourself.* The habits put forth are aimed at those of you who want to make at least some of your own investing decisions, although they can also help you ask the right questions of a professional adviser and analyze the performance of a fund manager.

RELATIVES ON THE BOOKSHELF

This book is intended as a stand-alone book. But it is also intended to dovetail with my series *The 100 Best Stocks to Buy* (coauthored with Scott Bobo), which is updated and published annually. In that series I apply most of these principles and habits to selecting the *100 Best Stocks*. Therefore, if you want to see these habits in action, go there. If you came from reading a *100 Best Stocks* book, you'll find more here on how I selected them and how you can do it yourself. Either way, these books can work on their own but are really meant to be together.

The Three Cycles of Investing

Now, we get to a few words on the actual anatomy of *The 25 Habits of Highly Successful Investors*. In crafting *25 Habits*, I felt it important to group or categorize the habits according to the three main activities you'll do as an investor:

- *Developing your investing style.* As an investor, the first and most comprehensive "thing" you do is to develop an investing style. Every investing style is different, for every investor has different needs and perceives how an investment meets those needs differently. If all investors did the same thing to achieve the same goals, there would be no real market; all money would flow to a few specific investments (which wouldn't really happen, because nobody would sell them). Your style is a foundation, applied over and over and based on your needs, risk tolerance, and time, and added to by experience. You'll develop and use some information and analytic tools along the way to make your style work better. I group six habits in *Part I: Style for Success.*

• *Buying a security.* What most of us think about when we think about investing is the actual selection and purchase of a security—as addressed in this book mainly, investing in a *stock.* Here, you learn repeatable approaches for buying a stock like you're buying the whole business, basing the decision on fundamentals, intangibles, and price. Twelve "buy" habits are presented as *Part II: Appraise for Success.*

• *Owning a security.* What fewer investors think about—or at least, what they tend not to form good habits around—is what to do with a stock, that share of a business, once they buy it. How do you keep track? How do you verify that your investment is still the best place for your money? How do you manage the investment to maximize your return from it? When do you sell? These are all questions a small business buyer would ask about owning the business. The final seven habits are presented in *Part III: Own for Success.*

Ready? Here we go.

PART I

STYLE FOR SUCCESS:
CRAFTING YOUR INDIVIDUAL INVESTING STYLE

Some very talented and intuitive people can pick up a golf club and tee off without a hitch. Or they stand behind a podium and get their speech right the first time, right off the bat (pardon the mixed sports analogy). Don't you hate them? For the rest of us, it takes some preparation to start and to feel good about doing something. We want to learn and think about it, and know the ropes (oops, there I go again) before we try. Eventually we all seek a reliable, repeatable style. Over time, we "get the feel," and expect our style to improve. The same applies to golf, public speaking—and investing.

Part I provides six habits covering important techniques and thoughts to help you initiate—and refine—your own personal investing style.

HABIT 1

Know Yourself— and Know What to Expect

It's a warm Friday evening, and you've settled in to watch *Sleepless in Seattle* or some other classic favorite movie on your DVD machine. Just as you hit the "Play" button, your cell phone quacks at you. It's one of your old college buddies, Josh.

He asks you to go whitewater rafting tomorrow. "It's going to be hot. You'll love it. C'mon, give it a try."

Uh, huh. Yeah, right.

You hate cold water. Really, you don't like water, period, and you especially don't like being in it. You don't like slippery rocks. You're not sure you're up to the inevitable splash fights or free-fall (or so it seems) rapids or other chances you might take. And the mosquitoes and harsh sun—not to mention the potentially uncomfortable and silly chatter of old buddies of an era gone by.

But it does kinda sound like fun, doesn't it? Might be just the thing for a hot day, and to reconnect with your buds. You might not only get a kick out of it, but also find a new activity and pleasure and something new for the future.

You *should* do it.

What do you do? What do you tell Josh?

Like most great adventures in life—at least those not entirely within your profession, your personality, or your daily comfort zone—you might step back for a second to review who you are, what you like, and what you expect to gain (or lose) if you say "yes."

You'll have to decide if the pleasure is worth the effort, cost, or possible discomfort you might experience along the way. Is the gain worth the pain? That, of course, is the bottom line.

Perhaps it's a bit of a stretch to compare investing with a summer weekend rafting trip, but in some ways they're similar. When you're investing, you know that from time to time:

- You'll get wet.
- You'll get scared.
- You'll be uncomfortable.

But, you'll experience the thrill of success and accomplishment along the way. And, your financial future is likely to be more secure as a result.

With both adventures, you'll want to think about the probable outcomes. You'll want to keep the entire adventure within your comfort zone. You'll want to imagine what you will get out of it, and how much and how often you'll get wet along the way.

You'll want to think about what's reasonable to expect over the long term, what the realistic outcomes are, and decide whether the reward is worth the risk. As you would with any adventure, personal or professional, good investors habitually:

- Sense the outcomes.
- Sense the risks.
- Set reasonable expectations.

- Stay within themselves.
- Take what the markets give them.

Good investors, by habit, have a healthy and balanced view of what they're about to undertake.

Know What You're Trying to Accomplish

Why invest? That's the first question any prudent investor must answer.

Investing isn't about bragging rights, nor do you invest "because everyone else is doing it." A prudent investor invests to enhance the growth of personal income and wealth over a period of time. By buying a stock or fund or bond, you wisely deploy your personal capital into the capital markets to achieve a return—nothing less and nothing more.

In your profession, you earn income. Over time, if your finances are well managed, you'll save some of that income. Investing is (or should be) done to produce some return in the form of current income and/or growth, of that savings. Eventually, as you age, investment growth and income overtake your current earnings in size and importance, and if all goes well they should produce more than your then-current income after you retire.

In a nutshell: *Make it, keep it, grow it.*

These six simple words really are what personal finance and wealth management are all about. Investing essentially covers the "grow it" part. If you make it but can't keep it, you'll have nothing for the future. If you make it and keep it but can't grow it, you're likely to consume whatever "seed corn" you have and deplete your savings. Investing should guard against that outcome.

So a big part of Habit 1 is to deploy *make it, keep it, grow it* in your personal finances.

Know What's Realistic

Do people make millions in the market? Sure. But not very many, at least not very many mortal individuals like you or me, right? People make millions on lottery tickets, too, but even fewer—too few to really matter—attain their wealth this way.

As an investor, you should develop the habit of having reasonable expectations. Baseball provides a good analogy: sure, you can swing for the fences to try to hit home runs, but you'll strike out a lot, and the home runs will likely be too few and far between to be of any consequence for the team.

If you have reasonable expectations—and stay within those expectations—you'll likely come out ahead. As a baseball hitter, you'll get fewer home runs, perhaps, but a lot more singles, doubles, and the occasional triple. As a whitewater rafter, you won't get wet as often, and you'll enjoy the raft trip more. You won't have to deal with the pain and ambiguity of being dumped in the rapids—in financial terms, of major failure—quite as often. Your investments, while always needing some attention and upkeep, won't keep you up at night.

Investing Returns—and Their Alternatives

So what *is* a reasonable return to expect from your investments?

That's a tough question these days, especially as volatility has increased and markets can turn up or down seemingly on a dime. Beyond that, we all hear about the increased cost of things we save for long term, such as retirement or a college education, and we panic at the idea that our savings just won't reach far enough. We start to feel as if anything less than a 20 percent annual return won't do.

Knowing what you can expect is critical, not only for planning your long-term finances but also for understanding alternatives. What do I mean by "alternatives?"

Any investor should know the alternatives, and should invest only when investing is the best and most prudent alternative. If the stock market indicates a 5 percent return but you can earn 6 percent with a virtually free bank CD or 7 percent (implied) by paying off all or part of your mortgage, these alternatives must be taken seriously for at least *part* of your investible capital. Similarly, within the world of investing, an investment that can deliver, say, 10 or 20 percent returns with greater risk must be compared with alternatives earning 2 or 3 percent with relatively lower risk.

Good investors get in the habit of constantly evaluating alternatives. (See Habit 24: Sell When There's Something Better to Buy.) Good investors are also in the habit of using a moderate, *achievable* investment return as an assumption for the future growth of their wealth.

Reasonable Returns—Over the Years

Back to the current question: What *should* you expect from your investments? What *is* "achievable?"

For years, the rule of thumb offered by the financial community for stock market returns was 10 percent. Data collected from the 1920s until about 2000 bore this out—market performance plus dividend payouts came pretty close to 10 percent.

Now, how can a stock market, which really is a sum of the values of all corporations traded in that market, return 10 percent per year when the total economy, measured by Gross Domestic Product (GDP) is growing say, between 2 and 4 percent a year? Does this make sense? Can corporations, taken as a whole, grow faster than the economy as a whole? And, if so, is this sustainable?

These are great questions, and all investors should wrap their heads around the answers. In fact, stock market investing returns have outperformed the economy as a whole over the long haul, but not by as much as the numbers might suggest.

Furthermore, it appears that the rule-of-thumb 10 percent return has moderated. Today it's closer to 7 to 8 percent. Where did the 10 percent come from? There were three components:

- GDP growth—real economic growth—averaging 3 percent
- Inflation—averaging perhaps 3–4 percent over the long haul
- Dividends and payouts—cash earned and paid out by companies and not retained as part of the company's value. The average payout, at least for S&P 500 stocks is just over 2 percent.

If you add these figures, you get to the 8 or 9 percent range. The final 1 to 2 percent (to reach 10 percent total) is probably attributable to large publicly traded companies doing an increased share of total business, as they force smaller competitors and mom-and-pops aside. So the 10 percent figure, so long as this market share gain was intact and so long as the economy as a whole pulled forward in the 2 to 4 percent range, made sense.

Today, however, economic growth as measured by GDP has waned somewhat, and that market share growth has probably also waned. Many companies are seeing renewed competition from smaller, more nimble firms, especially as larger firms downsize and outsource more of their business. A rather dramatic case in point (pardon the pun) is offered by the beer industry, where big is no longer best and market share enjoyed by the larger brewers is reverting back to small brewers, microbrewers, and so forth.

So what is "reasonable" to expect today?

Here's a number: from 1929 through 2011, as measured by the S&P 500 index as a broad indicator of all stock market performance, the stock markets have gained 5.1 percent per year, compounded, over that 83-year term. As a real number, it implicitly includes inflation effects, market share gains, etc. Add to that the 2.2 percent or so in dividends, and you get to a 7.3 percent annualized return for stocks.

That's nice—7.3 percent, versus something less than 1 percent these days for most savings accounts, and even a paltry 1.5 percent for government bonds—who wouldn't want to be in stocks? Well, the answer is simple—that 7.3 percent comes with considerable variation, or as market pros call it, *volatility*, from one year to the next.

In fact, in only 14 of the 83 years, the S&P 500 did grow in single digits. That means that in 69 of the 83 years, the change was something larger or smaller! How could any investor sleep at night?

While this sounds awful, there is some good news. First, some 55 of the 83 years are positive. Second, 46 of the 83 years are within a relatively benign 0 to 30 percent range—if you think of it as rolling dice, most of the outcomes are positive, and most are better than the 5.1 percent long term average. Still, in the really bad years, in the 1930s and more recently 2008, things can get really bad, and those assaults and corrections can really "ding" the averages.

Good investors are aware of these figures, and should be quite happy with 5 percent growth with some current payout, in the 2 percent range. It's reasonable to expect a little bit more—but 20 percent a year ongoing is simply not realistic.

Know Yourself

Back to that rafting analogy presented at the beginning of the chapter. Assuming you find any of the pleasures of rafting worthwhile at all, what are you willing to risk to entertain those pleasures? If you're a risk taker, you probably don't mind finding yourself in the river once in a while in exchange for a chance to enjoy the thrills of speed and action. Spills for thrills, right?

Most rafters, on the other hand, wouldn't mind getting wet occasionally to enjoy the adventure, the camaraderie, and the cooling refreshment on a hot day—but don't want to be pitched headfirst into an ice-cold, swirling, rock-infested rapids. In the investing space, most investors are willing to put up with a down day here and there as part of the process of reaping decent gains and finding a winner here or there, but aren't comfortable risking large amounts or enduring painful declines for a chance to double, triple, or quadruple their cash overnight.

IT'S INVESTING, NOT TRADING

Investing isn't (or shouldn't be) gambling. It is taking calculated, prudent risks to achieve decent returns over time. Overnight or short-term windfalls are nice, but they aren't the goal. Similarly, investors don't buy and sell, buy and sell, hoping to capture a short-term gain. That's *trading.* Trading isn't necessarily gambling, but it is typically playing in the market as a professional securities dealer would, buying and selling, buying and selling, trying to capture small opportunities in the market over and over. Trading isn't necessarily a bad thing—if you have the time, energy, and expertise to pull it off. But it isn't the mainstream activity of those who read this book. This book is about the habits of the *investor,* not the trader.

So who are you, as an investor? What kinds of risks are you willing to take? Would you rather have $5 in hand or a 10 percent chance at winning $50? It's important to know what makes you feel good and particularly, what makes you feel *bad* as an investor. You want to know yourself, and you want to stay within your comfort zone as an investor. If you don't, you might end up doing dumb things, just like you might do on the rafting trip. If you're the type who prefers to avoid falling out of the boat at all costs, and you fall out anyway, that can set your confidence back for years, if not forever.

You can assess your own tolerance for risk by envisioning what might happen in the markets and how you might react to it. How would you deal with a ten percent decline in your investments? A 20 percent decline? A year like 2008, where the S&P 500 dropped some 38 percent, almost all of it in the last four months of the year?

Your past life experiences will tell you something about your risk tolerance and risk profile. When seeking your job, spouse, your place to live, the car you bought, or for that matter, any purchase, did you balance bigger rewards against some significant risk or uncertainty? Or do you tend to seek the "sure thing," the "safe bet," the choice with a little more predictability at the expense of pleasure? Of course, some people are willing to take more risks socially or with their life-styles than they are with their money, so even this test isn't a sure bet to determine who you are as an investor.

There are tools out there to help appraise your risk as an investor. They measure your willingness to risk loss for the promise of a larger gain. I recommend taking a short risk assessment quiz available from Rutgers University at *www .njaes.rutgers.edu/money/riskquiz/*; there are lots of others out there too.

Of course, outside of a thrill seeker or habitual gambler, nobody takes risks unless there is some reward. The reward of a 7 percent, 8 percent, even a 10 percent return versus leaving your money in a bank is substantial and worthwhile. So part of the process of investing is to understand not only your toler-ance for risk but also the rewards that might accrue to you if you take it. In Habit 2: Know and Use Basic Investing Math,

I'll show the substantial rewards of earning even just a little bit more per year on your money.

Invest What You Can Afford to Lose

If you're a "sleep at night" investor, you may only put at risk what you can afford to lose in a worst-case scenario; you'll leave your other powder dry in the form of cash savings, your home, and so forth. Prudent investors shouldn't invest to the point where vital cash reserves, a car, a home, or a college fund must be tapped into to put food on the table.

You may find that it helps to tier, your investments (as I'll describe later in Habit 5: Segment, or "Tier," Your Portfolio) into smaller segments. For example, you can create a smaller pool of "risk" capital invested for higher returns that you can easily afford to lose; combine this with other larger segments of your portfolio engaged in such a way as to make losses less likely. The 10 percent you could easily afford to lose is invested differently than the next, say, 20 percent. Losing that larger portion would be a little more painful, so you invest it in lower-risk stocks.

Make Sure Everyone's in the Boat

The examples given so far focus on *you* as an individual investor. That's fine—if you're the only individual involved and only your capital is at risk. But last time I checked, the majority of Americans of investing age are married and/or have some sort of family; the money isn't all yours. Read the memo before it wrecks your household. Unless you're explicitly declared CEO of your family's investments, take the time to check out the risk profiles and preferences of others in your family unit. Make sure they're on board with the objectives, what returns are reasonable, and what risks might be taken to achieve them.

I'll take that back. Even if you *are* the "investing CEO," it's still a good idea to check. You might have differing ideas of what you can afford to lose. In any event, if everyone is on the same page about investing objectives and risks, you're far less likely to be thrown in the water by a family member, and your investing life will probably proceed much more smoothly.

Get Into the Habit

- Know what you're trying to accomplish. Say it out loud, discuss it with your family, and write it down.
- Know what's realistic to expect.
- Decide if you are happy meeting, exceeding, or staying slightly under market returns, given the risk and energy involved.
- Invest what you can afford to lose.
- Make sure everyone in your family is on board.

HABIT 2

Know and Use Basic Investing Math

OMG. Yikes. Yuck. Eee-eeeek. Oh, boy, here it comes. Math. That four-letter word that conjures up eighth-grade algebraic misery and general boredom and worse from your past.

And we're only on Habit 2; will it get worse from here?

Okay, okay. Nothing to fret, nothing to be fearful of. No equations to memorize, no painful homework, no pop quizzes or chapter-ending tests, here. And I promise I'll try not to mention the word "math" again in any of the subsequent twenty-three habits.

But I do think, as an investor, that it's important to understand a few simple math principles—ones that will build your purpose and philosophy of investing and motivate you to achieve more. These principles become part of your automatic thought process—a habit, really—and make it easier to understand what you're doing and why.

We'll keep it simple. Good cooks know how to use garlic in their cooking, but stop short of knowing the concentration and chemistry of allyl propyl disulfide, the primary active ingredient. I won't bore you with algebraic details either—only the results. These math principles are your "garlic." You'll use them over and over without the need to take them apart. As Warren Buffett once said, "If calculus were required, I'd have to go back to delivering papers."

"The Greatest Mathematical Discovery of All Time"

The first stop on our short mathematical side trip is at the concept of *compounding*. Compounding is what happens when an investment earns a return in a given year. Rather than being withdrawn, that return is allowed to stay invested, or reinvested elsewhere, so that it too, in addition to your original investment, earns a return.

Suppose, for instance, you invest $1,000, and earn $50 on that investment in the first year—a 5 percent return, for those of you paying attention. You reinvest that $50 either in the same investment or in another earning 5 percent. At the end of the second year, you'll earn not just another $50 on the original $1,000 invested, but also $2.50 on the $50 earned in the first year. You'll have $1,102.50—the original $1,000, plus the $50 earned each year on the original $1,000, plus the $2.50 you earned on the $50 you earned in the first year.

Whew. I feel you already looking at the clock, waiting for that magical end to this short math class.

Suppose you have more money to invest and more time—much more than two years—to let these returns earn even more as time goes on. You earn 5 percent now on $52.50 from year one, plus the $50 from year two, and so forth. In fact, after five years, on that first $50 you earn you would be up to earning not just 5 percent but the equivalent of more that 27 percent of that amount, or about $13. You'd have four years of compounded earnings on the second $50, three years on the third $50, and so forth. In fact, in total, your original investment would have grown to $1,276—the original $1,000, plus the nominal $50 or 5 percent earned each year, plus the compounded interest.

Okay, so maybe this hasn't grabbed you yet, and what's coming next may perpetuate the pain just a bit. But it will get pretty interesting (no pun intended) in just a minute.

It's time for a formula, a basic formula of investing that everyone should know, but you won't be doing daily calculations as you read the stock pages. I promise. It's the concept that's important (I know, you never bought that phrase when your math teacher tried it on you, either!).

Anyway, here goes:

The future value of an invested sum, that is, what it will be worth after n number of years, is the present value (the sum invested today) times $(1 + i)^n$, where i is the rate of return, the 5 percent used earlier, and the exponent n is the number of years the investment is allowed to ride, or:

Future Value (FV) = Present Value (PV) $* (1 + i)^n$

So, in our example, we invested $1,000 (PV) at 5 percent (i) for 5 years (n). Mathematically, that's $1,000 times (1.05) times (1.05) times (1.05) times (1.05), times (1.05), arriving at the $1,276 noted above.

So big deal, you might say. A scary exponent and a formula, and you end up with only $26 more than the "simple" $50 added on each year. Now, here is where the "power" (again no pun intended) of the exponent comes in, the power that led Albert Einstein to call compounding "the greatest mathematical discovery of all time."

Here's the point: If you leave that compounding machine on for, say, fifteen, twenty, thirty, even forty years, the results can be amazing, especially if you're compounding a relatively strong return rate. To illustrate, here is a table showing what happens to $100,000 invested for n number of years at an i rate of return:

FIGURE 2.1: COMPOUNDED GROWTH OF $100,000 INVESTED

Compounded Growth of $100,000

Number of Years:	1	2	5	10	15	20	25	30	40
1.0%	$101,000	$102,010	$105,101	$110,462	$116,097	$122,019	$128,243	$134,785	$148,886
2.0%	$102,000	$104,040	$110,408	$121,899	$134,587	$148,595	$164,061	$181,136	$220,804
3.0%	$103,000	$106,090	$115,927	$134,392	$155,797	$180,611	$209,378	$242,726	$326,204
4.0%	$104,000	$108,160	$121,665	$148,024	$180,094	$219,112	$266,584	$324,340	$480,102
5.0%	$105,000	$110,250	$127,628	$162,889	$207,893	$265,330	$338,635	$432,194	$703,999
6.0%	$106,000	$112,360	$133,823	$179,085	$239,656	$320,714	$429,187	$574,349	$1,028,572
7.0%	$107,000	$114,490	$140,255	$196,715	$275,903	$386,968	$542,743	$761,226	$1,497,446
8.0%	$108,000	$116,640	$146,933	$215,892	$317,217	$466,096	$684,848	$1,006,266	$2,172,452
9.0%	$109,000	$118,810	$153,862	$236,736	$364,248	$560,441	$862,308	$1,326,768	$3,140,942
10.0%	$110,000	$121,000	$161,051	$259,374	$417,725	$672,750	$1,083,471	$1,744,940	$4,525,926
11.0%	$111,000	$123,210	$168,506	$283,942	$478,459	$806,231	$1,358,546	$2,289,230	$6,500,087
12.0%	$112,000	$125,440	$176,234	$310,585	$547,357	$964,629	$1,700,006	$2,995,992	$9,305,097
13.0%	$113,000	$127,690	$184,244	$339,457	$625,427	$1,152,309	$2,123,054	$3,911,590	$13,278,155
14.0%	$114,000	$129,960	$192,541	$370,722	$713,794	$1,374,349	$2,646,192	$5,095,016	$18,888,351
15.0%	$115,000	$132,250	$201,136	$404,556	$813,706	$1,636,654	$3,291,895	$6,621,177	$26,786,355

Now, perhaps, I'll have your undivided attention, and now, maybe, you'll see the magic. You may even conclude that this investing math thing isn't so bad.

Take a look at what happens to that $100,000 invested at 5 percent in Year 1. It's worth $105,000—no surprise, right? But after fifteen years, what happens? It doubles. After thirty years, it's more than four times your original investment. And that's without adding a single dime to the investment; you're just letting it ride from one year to the next.

You don't have to imagine what happens if you earn a bit more on your investments—that's right in front of you in this table. Earn 15 percent for forty years? *Now, let's not always see the same hands.* Your investment—bottom right corner—would grow to more than $26 million! This, incidentally, illustrates how Warren Buffett became the second wealthiest American—his Berkshire Hathaway investment has earned more than 30 percent annually for forty years.

And you can only imagine what would happen if you added some savings to the $100,000 each year, instead of just "letting it ride." Save, invest, grow. *Make it, keep it, grow it.* You can see the power, and think of it every time you work on your investments.

For a Few Dollars More

I dropped a subtle hint in the previous section: even beating the market by just a little, over time, can bring in a whole lot more money *in the long run*—because of compounding.

If you take a closer look at Figure 2.1, you would have seen that earning 6 percent, instead of 5 percent, over, say, fifteen, twenty or thirty years would accumulate a lot more wealth. You would earn almost $140,000 more after thirty years ($574,349 versus $432,194)—not bad for a mere 1 percent premium over the going "market" rate of return of 5 percent.

In fact, we'll take a closer look at what happens if you beat the market by just a percent or two, up to 5 percent over time, in Figure 2.2 below:

FIGURE 2.2: WHAT HAPPENS
WHEN YOU BEAT THE MARKET

Number of Years:	1	2	5	10	15
5% Market Return:	$105,000	$110,250	$127,628	$162,889	$207,893
Outperform by:					
1 %	$106,000	$112,360	$133,823	$179,085	$238,656
2 %	$107,000	$114,490	$140,255	$196,715	$275,903
3 %	$108,000	$116,640	$146,933	$215,892	$317,217
4 %	$109,000	$118,810	$153,862	$236,736	$364,248
5 %	$110,000	$121,000	$161,051	$259,374	$417,725

Number of Years:	20	25	30	40
5% Market Return:	$265,330	$338,635	$432,194	$703,999
Outperform by:				
1 %	$320,714	$429,187	$574,349	$1,028,572
2 %	$386,968	$542,743	$761,226	$1,497,446
3 %	$466,096	$684,848	$1,006,266	$2,172,452
4 %	$560,441	$862,308	$1,326,768	$3,140,942
5 %	$672,750	$1,083,471	$1,744,940	$4,525,926

Here you can plainly see what happens if you earn the "base" market return of 5 percent, and what happens if you beat that return, just by a percent or two, maybe a few percentage points, over time. Beat by just 3 percent, and the thirty-year return more than doubles from $432,194 to more than $1 million.

Of course, this all sounds great if you have thirty years to wait and if you can make 8 percent on your investments. Even if you can't, the potential rewards for earning just a little bit more are substantial. As an investor, trying to earn just a little more than market returns—not 10 or 20 or 50 percent more as many investors (or speculators!) try to—is developing a good and well-rewarded investing habit. Even a percent or two means a lot.

FOR A FEW DOLLARS *LESS*

We just examined the benefits of investing to earn just a little bit more than market returns. Of course, the converse is true, too. Be a little bit too conservative, and you may cost yourself a few percentage points in return. Sure, you can sleep at night, but what happens to long-term performance? Another table is suggested:

FIGURE 2.3: WHAT HAPPENS WHEN YOU UNDERPERFORM THE MARKET

Number of Years:	1	2	5	10
5% Market Return:	$105,000	$110,250	$127,628	$162,889
Underperform by:				
0.5%	$104,500	$109,203	$124,618	$155,297
1.0%	$104,000	$108,160	$121,665	$148,024
1.5%	$103,500	$107,123	$118,769	$141,060
2.0%	$103,000	$106,090	$115,927	$134,392
2.5%	$102,500	$105,063	$113,141	$128,008

FIGURE 2.3: WHAT HAPPENS WHEN YOU UNDERPERFORM THE MARKET—CONTINUED

Number of Years:	15	20	25	30	40
5% Market Return:	$207,893	$265,330	$338,635	$432,194	$703,999
Underperform by:					
0.5%	$193,528	$241,171	$300,543	$374,532	$581,636
1.0%	$180,094	$219,112	$266,584	$324,340	$480,102
1.5%	$167,535	$198,979	$236,324	$280,679	$395,926
2.0%	$155,797	$180,611	$209,378	$242,726	$326,204
2.5%	$144,830	$163,862	$185,394	$209,757	$268,506

Now, what happens when you earn, say, only 3.5 percent over time while the market as a whole is earning 5 percent? You'll end up with $280,679 after thirty years instead of $432,194. Sure, you might sleep better at night, and that's a decision that's up to you. But there is a cost.

You can imagine two further truths from Figure 2.3:

- Even a few years of negative returns can really derail the compounding train.
- The cost of management fees—for mutual funds or for private financial advisers and other investment managers—can be significant over time. If you pay a fund, or an adviser, 1 percent of asset value each year, that gives the same result as "underperforming" by 1 percent, which can cost about $13,500 after just fifteen years ($193,528–$180,094). That doesn't mean it's a bad idea, but it does mean that you should understand the true cost.

Fast Figuring: The Rule of 72

As mentioned earlier, no investor in the history of the world understands, or has applied, the principle of compounding to a greater degree and with more success than Warren Buffett. Yet he (and many other investors) reportedly does most investing math without a calculator. Does he possess a 2-gigahertz mind that's able to grind out multiple power and exponential calculations faster than you can say Coca-Cola? Hardly. Not to say that being the gifted individual that he is, he couldn't perform quite a few rapid-fire calculations in his head. But he doesn't. Instead, he uses one of the most useful general rules in investing, maybe in all mathematics, as a computational shortcut. It's known as the Rule of 72.

Even if you hate math, you'll want to turn the Rule of 72 into one of your favorite investing habits. It will help you do a lot of things, and you'll amaze people at the next cocktail party you attend!

The Rule of 72 is based on compounding mathematics. With the Rule of 72 you can very quickly and precisely estimate two things: (1) the rate of return needed to double a sum of money within a time period, or (2) the time period needed to double a sum of money, given a rate of return. Stated more simply, if you know the rate of return, you can compute the time period, and if you know the time period, you can compute the approximate rate of return:

- The number of years to double an investment at a given return rate:
    = 72 divided by the rate of return (as an integer: the rate × 100)

- The return rate required to double an investment over a given number of years:
    = 72 divided by the number of years

Examples will help:

- At 12 percent, it takes six years to double your money (72 divided by 12).
- To double your money in eight years, you must earn a 9 percent rate of return (72 divided by 8).
- At 10 percent, how many years does it take to quadruple your money? Answer: It doubles in 7.2 years (72 divided by 10), so quadrupling would take twice that long, or 14.4 years.
- If your best friend brags about having bought a house for $150,000 that's now worth $600,000 and he's had it for ten years, what is the rate of return? Answer: It doubled twice ($150K to $300K to $600K) in ten years, or once every five years. So (72 divided by 5) gives a 14.4 percent compounded rate of return. Not bad at all, but as a sharp investor you might have beaten your friend in the stock market! Not to mention impressing him or her by doing this calculation in your head!

GETTING RETURN RATES RIGHT

Just what is the rate of return on an investment? It depends on how it's calculated. Take a look at the example just presented for the Rule of 72. Your friend bragged about buying a house for $150,000 and selling it ten years later for $600,000. He or she might call that a 300 percent return and, because it occurred over ten years, boasting of an average of 30 percent per year. On the surface, that's correct.

But when evaluating the home purchase as an investment (compared to other investments), you must include the compounding effect to have an accurate, apples-to-apples comparison. If that $150,000 were invested ten years ago, with compounding, what rate of return would have produced $600,000? As approximated using the Rule of 72 above, the compounded rate of return is 14.4 percent, not 30 percent. Still not bad, but you'll have to compare it with other compound returns available from other investments, as well as the risks with those investments.

In Habit 1, I introduced the long-term market return rate of 5.1 percent—that's a compounded rate of return, which implicitly assumes that investment returns are reinvested going forward. The calculation is similar to the 14.4 percent return on the house, which as we all know, is unlikely anyway in today's real estate market.

Okay, that's it—class dismissed. You may have really grooved on this stuff, or it may have made your eyes glaze over (either way, you're invited to stay after class to wipe off the white board). Even without the detail, if you picked up the importance of compounding as a concept, and how just a little bit more return over just a little bit more time can really help your investments, you'll be ahead of the investing game from now on.

Get Into the Habit

- Always remember the power of compounding.
- Strive to make "just a few dollars more."
- Know the true cost of professional management and fund fees.
- Practice your "Rule of 72" shorthand. It comes in handy, and you can impress your friends too!
- Think in terms of *compounded* rates of return—it's more conservative and more realistic.

HABIT 3

Get the Right—
and Right Amount of—Information

Successful investors base their investing on information. That's not too hard to comprehend, for investing not based on information is hardly more than guesswork, right?

The highly successful investor (or any other investor, as distinguished from a guesser or a gambler) stays tuned in to the business and financial world. Now, for most of you reading *The 25 Habits of Highly Successful Investors*, investing isn't your full-time occupation. Far from it, probably.

So the real imperative is to stay tuned in to events, results, and analysis flowing from or about companies you might own or want to own, from the business world, and about the economy as a whole. You want to "drip irrigate" yourself with the highlights, the important stuff, and an occasional in-depth article close to your centers of interest. You don't want to be surprised. Beyond that, you want to have access to the information you need when it comes time to do a deeper investigation—say, to add a company to your portfolio.

Know What You Need to Know

Investing information comes in all shapes and sizes from all media and sources. These range from venerable and focused financial journals such as the *Wall Street Journal* to more tangential sources like the evening news or company publicity or even your neighbor across the street.

The key is to know what you need to know, and tune in so that you can get enough without being overwhelmed with the proverbial fire hose of today's Information Age.

As we move into Part II and Part III of *25 Habits*, where we cover more specific habits related to acquiring and owning investments, the specific pieces of information you should seek will become clearer. For now, suffice it to say there are five basic kinds of information. Your other investing habits, as you adopt them and refine them, will determine the specifics.

1. *Economic trends.* What is going on in the global economy that might directly or indirectly affect your investments? Employment reports, interest rates, debt problems, political crises, and banking crises will affect your investments as a whole. When the news is bad you might want to get more defensive or take a breather altogether. Global news can also affect individual investment decisions. For example, the European banking crisis and recession will affect a U.S. company selling a lot of goods and services in Europe.

2. *Industry trends.* If you're investing in the food or chemical or auto or defense industries, it pays to keep up with the latest global and domestic news in these industries. In some industries, like the food processing or airline industries, you will want to keep up with trends in *adjacent* industries affecting performance, for example, agriculture and agriculture prices for the food processing industry and energy and oil prices for the airlines.

3. *Financial stuff.* As I'll explain further in in Part II, you'll need access to company financial statements and figures to make good decisions whether to buy a business (i.e., a stock) or keep a business. Revenues, expenses, profits, cash flows, assets, and liabilities broadly categorize what you're looking for. You'll need to tap into the latest updates, as well as history and historical trends.

COMPANY NEWS AND MARKET NEWS AREN'T THE SAME

If you ask someone or search for news about a particular company, you'll often come up with articles highlighting the price of a stock and its recent movements. "Company XYZ hit a fifty-two-week high and has traded in the range of $25.50 to $42.90 . . . blah, blah, blah." You'll see a lot of quotes, charts, price history, technical analysis of price movements, and so forth. Is this what you're looking for when you seek financial news about a company? No, but it's easier to write about. It just goes to show that the Internet is full of meaningless articles and sites that focus on what's happening with a company as a *stock* as opposed to what's happening with a company as a *business.*

Learn to distinguish between the two.

1. *Soft stuff.* When I say "soft stuff" I am referring to the more intangible characteristics of a business or a company, like brand, market position and dynamics (meaning marketplace, not "stock" market), management and leadership, public perception, and various subtle strengths and weaknesses that foretell the *future* (whereas financials mostly describe the past.)

2. *Analysis.* Most of the previous items are directed toward an ongoing "drip irrigation" of facts and updates that, as a prudent investor, will keep you on top of things. When you "go shopping" to add something to your portfolio, do

a regular analysis of your investments (Habit 25). You will want a more detailed analysis of a business, taken in part from your own sources of facts, figures, and soft stuff, but augmented by useful analysis and fact gathering by pros. Prudent investors will supplement their own analysis with professional work; as we'll see shortly, the *Value Line Investment Survey* brings together a lot of information in a concise and useful format.

WHY USE PROFESSIONAL INVESTMENT ANALYSIS?

As we agreed at the outset of *25 Habits*, you're an individual investor, in charge of your own investments, and you're smart and savvy enough to make your own investing decisions. That said, you shouldn't ignore the advice of the pros, particularly the well-established and unbiased (that is, not linked to any trading operation or brokerage) reviews of a company such as *Value Line*. Why? Two reasons, mainly: (1) to save time and (2) like it or not, despite what the "ideal" world might suggest, not everything there is to know about a company is readily available to the public, i.e., *you*. *Value Line* and other analysts have contacts within the company who will answer specific questions that you, Mr. Individual Investor, would never get a chance to ask.

It's a Balance

We've established that you're not a professional investor. You have neither the time, budget, nerves, nor stomach to spend sixteen hours a day glued to the newswires and various investment services to feed top to bottom on every scrap of business and market news that spews forth. You want enough to be smart and prudent, without drowning in the information overload that would inevitably result from staying *too* connected.

Every investor—as a habit—will want to experiment with different information sources and information-gathering routines. The idea is to get not too much and not too little info, but just the right amount. Enough to stay informed, enough resources to dig deeper when necessary, as when something important is happening. *But not too much.*

Why not too much? Because you'll get burned out. Not only that—if you take in too much, the important stuff may not stand out as it should. Over time you'll learn to read more frequently about dynamic companies and industries in your portfolio. You'll find out where big-picture and company-specific news appears regularly and where it's less frequent— maybe weekly, instead of daily. You'll learn where to find out about more stable companies and industries in your portfolio, such as food and food processing.

Remember—less is usually more. If you learn to concentrate on a few sources and read them regularly, you're likely to get more out of them.

The whole point is to establish a set of reliable, consistent information sources and a routine to use and make the most of them. You'll want to experiment with new ones along the way, but in all cases, you'll seek value—that is, the most utility for the time (and sometimes, money) invested.

Regular, and Other, Reads

Without going into the specifics of each source or media venue, here is a list of what I think are the better sources, grouped by category:

- Economic trends:
  - *Wall Street Journal*
  - *New York Times business section, especially Sunday*
  - *Nightly Business Report (PBS)*
  - *Morning Edition, especially Business News (NPR)*
  - *The Economist magazine*
  - *Finance portals such as Yahoo!Finance (finance.yahoo*
    .com), Google Finance (finance.google.com)
- Industry trends—be creative here;
  - *Wall Street Journal, especially "Marketplace" section*
  - *Business Week and other magazines/news portals*
  - *Industry publications. An assortment of monthly, and some*
    weekly, news magazines and newsletters targeted to industry
    professionals is available. Try Design News for technology
    (www.designnews.com), Automotive Week (www.autoweek
    .com) for the auto industry, or almost any other such pub-
    lication (just do a search on "XYZ industry"). It's amaz-
    ing how much is free, but you may have to pay for the best
    sources.
  - *"Smart friends." Do you have a friend or relative in*
    the business? That's a good place to get some insight—
    although, recognize that from time to time such a source
    might be biased or may be restricted by confidentiality
    requirements. That said, if you have a friend in the semi-
    conductor industry, that could be a valuable place to cap-
    ture the latest industry trends and understand the econom-
    ics of, say, "DRAM" (dynamic random access memories) or
    "SSHDs" (solid state hard drives) or some other industry-
    specific item.
  - *Street observations. What you see, day to day on the street,*
    can often signal what is going on in an industry. Big mark-
    downs or promotional campaigns (like "zero percent financ-
    ing") can suggest softness in an industry, just as long lines

and huge crowds can indicate the opposite (been to an Apple Store lately?).

- Financial stuff—now for the more "traditional" investing information:
  - *Financial portals—and "financial statements" pages*
  - *Company websites—most companies are doing a much better job these days than previously of making key financial reports available online (under "Investor Relations" tab or something similar). Look for annual reports (usually as PDF files), quarterly and annual filings including the more complete "10-K" annual report, and presentations for investor conferences.*
  - *Conference calls—listen to what the company has to say about itself as earnings and other financials (and a lot of intangibles) are presented.*
  - *Brokerage sites—you can usually work your way towards summary financials through the "Research" or similar sections of a broker website.*
  - *Analysis—Value Line summaries and similar services produce good financial summaries, sometimes improved by making their own judgments as to what is consistent over time as a reporting basis for, say, earnings per share, discounting or including one-time charges.*

- *Soft Stuff*—Again, you need to be creative. Many of the same sources work as for Industry Trends; only now the articles may be more about specific companies. Look also at (or listen to):
  - *Company website—how does the company view itself? Present itself?*
  - *Company presentations—to analysts and investor conferences (again, see the company website).*
  - *Company conference calls—get not only the facts and financials but also the tone and manner of management, small*

nuances and shifts in business strategy, the message behind the numbers—the reasons why the past did or didn't work and a view of the future.

- *Heard on the street—again, how the general public (customers, channel partners like retailers, etc.) views a company can tell a lot.*

- *Analysis*—this can be a "get what you pay for" scenario.
  - *Value Line—is still the best source I've seen for the individual investor. The subscription is a bit over $500 annually but it can often (less often, it's true, these days) be found in libraries or brokerage offices. (Consider sharing with an investor/friend!)*
  - *Brokerage analysis—Most online brokers offer a research section, and within those sections are reports compiled by paid analysts inside or outside the company. Be careful to avoid reports that are outdated; many also lead the reader to take an action in line with the brokerage's bias; even though this has improved in recent years, "buy" recommendations still outweigh others substantially. Brokerage recommendations also tend to capture what has already happened as opposed to what will; many "buy" recommendations come well after a stock has made its best moves. Be careful.*

What to Avoid

After the description of brokerage analysis offered in the last section, you're probably not surprised to see this subheading. Actually, most mainstream information sources are pretty good; you'll just have to navigate and experiment your way through to find your best value for the time and money invested.

As a rule, I avoid most of what I see on brokerage sites, and I avoid the flood of articles written for less name-branded sites like "Wall Street Cheat Sheet" and others, which either repeat stories found elsewhere on the web or bury you in meaningless information like a stock's trading range, volume, and whether it crossed its 200-day moving average last week. "Seeking Alpha" is the only one of these sites that I look at occasionally, although it appears that many less-than-seasoned investors produce some of these articles, too.

Find the news; avoid the noise.

WHAT WORKS FOR YOURS TRULY. . .

. . . is what works for me but it isn't necessarily what works for everyone. Personally, I keep up with one financial portal (Google Finance) several times during business hours and occasionally on a weekend. Through the portal, I follow some of the news stories, particularly from reputable news sources such as *Forbes* or newswire services like Reuters that come through the portal. I read the *Wall Street Journal* when I can. I watch *Nightly Business Report* when I can. *The Economist* got to be too heavy, but I am considering a return to its valuable insights on the global economy and occasionally on specific industries. I like to look at company websites. I keep *Value Line* at my disposal for more detailed analysis and its weekly summaries. I listen in on conference calls (or read transcripts) for most companies that I hold.

I avoid stories that are more about the markets than about companies, and I spend about one hour a day, most of it in the morning, keeping up. (I'm on Pacific time, which makes early morning hours more meaningful for me than some of you.)

You'll find your own groove, and it won't be exactly like mine.

Get Into the Habit

- Decide how much time you have, and want to spend, staying informed.
- Think about what you need or want among the five categories: Economic Trends, Industry Trends, Financial Stuff, Soft Stuff, and Analysis.
- Review sources in each category and select based on their value.
- Review your choices occasionally; drop the ones that aren't adding much; try others on for size.
- Tap into informal networks—friends, family, and industry insiders.
- Share information sources with other investors or friends, to cut cost or leverage each other's time.

HABIT 4

Find Your Diversification Sweet Spot

"Diversification is for people who don't know what they're doing."
Know who said that? I'll give you one good guess. Yes, indeed, it was the greatest, most successful investor of all time: Warren Buffett.

Now wouldn't you think, with what you've read and heard over the years, that the world's most successful investor would, in fact, depend a lot on diversification? That Buffett would want to "cover all bases" and reduce the risk of a cataclysmic explosion in his portfolio?

Well, apparently not. He is, in fact, *so* good at this that he feels that he doesn't need to diversify just to reduce risk. Now, most of us mortals can hardly claim to be that good, so we do feel the need to diversify to some extent, to not put all our eggs in one basket or a series of risky baskets. And in fact, Buffett does too—he owns several companies in different industries with different risk profiles.

But he also would say that diversification for diversification's sake is more likely to water down your returns than improve them. That sort of strategy can more likely benefit financial advisers and others who make money off of your money.

Smart diversification means taking some steps to reduce risk, without watering down returns. It means not diversifying just for diversification's sake. It means:

- Not buying a mutual fund or exchange traded fund with as many as 1,800 holdings, which will inevitably—mathematically—only produce market returns or something less after management or transaction costs are deducted.
- Not buying too many stocks yourself for much the same reason.
- Not just diversifying by asset class (e.g., stocks, bonds, cash, commodities) but smartly within the class.
- Not buying overlapping funds where the holdings are similar.

The Diversification Paradox

Almost all industry media and "expert" opinions on investing start with the same inviolate, unassailable principle, presented as if gospel: diversify. That longer version of the principle goes something like this: The prudent investor will always look for ways to diversify his or her portfolio by buying multiple stocks or funds in different industries. That way, risk is minimized, and there is a greater chance of achieving market rates of return.

Okay, not bad. Most investors are satisfied with something at least close to market rates of return, and most of them want to sleep at night. The part about "a greater chance of achieving market rates of return" is actually true. But the simple mathematical fact is that the more stocks you put into your portfolio, the less the odds of you beating the market.

Think of the old probability models you studied in high school. If you toss a penny into the air, it comes down heads or tails. Fifty-fifty probability. Toss a few more pennies in the air, say six total, and the odds are you'll get three heads and three tails, maybe two and four, maybe one and five, maybe even all six heads. Probabilities decrease as you go to the extremes, but these outcomes are all plausible. Now throw 100,000 pennies into the air. What are the chances of all 100,000 coming up heads? Desperately small. This is an extreme case, but the point remains: the more stocks you have, the more likely your winners and losers will cancel each other out.

Suppose you hit a home run and score a 50 percent gain on a stock. If it's one of four stocks in your portfolio and all others break even, the portfolio gains on average 12.5 percent. If it's one of ten stocks, with all the others breaking even, the gain is only 5 percent. Holding too many stocks dilutes the gains of the winners. Combined with transaction costs and management fees, this phenomenon helps explain why some two-thirds of stock mutual funds underperform the market, as measured by the S&P 500 index.

But what about reducing risk? True, the more pennies you throw, the lower the odds that they will all come up tails. If the performance of your stocks is really random, then owning more stocks reduces the chance of beating market returns. The converse is also true: Owning many stocks reduces the chance of dramatically underperforming the market.

Remember, true investors aren't random stock pickers! They take the risk out by understanding the companies and their value, rather than by spreading the risk across more companies. Smart investors are focused investors who drive toward deep understanding of their investments without diluting possible returns through diversification. They see danger in owning too many investments, which may be beyond the scope of what they can manage or keep track of. Here's the paradox: Instead of reducing risk through diversification, your risk may actually increase as it becomes harder for you to follow the fortunes of so many businesses! That's why Buffett and others reject diversification per se as an investment strategy. They prefer to reduce risk by watching a few companies and investments more closely.

The Myth of Asset Allocation

Accompanying the diversification panacea in many investment advisory circles is the notion of asset allocation, that is, the distribution of your investments across broad investment classes such as stocks, bonds, cash, and commodities. Variations of this strategy will distribute these investments among "large cap, mid cap, small cap," and "growth versus value" choices.

These are broad groupings and speak nothing to what is contained in them. You'll hear suggestions that the ideal portfolio should consist of "60 percent stocks," making no mention of *which* stocks should make up the 60 percent. Is there any value here? Not much. It's good for brokers who want to create and present a lot of pie charts to clients, but it stops way short of being useful investment advice.

As well, you'll hear brokerage houses and investment advisers pronouncing recommendations to "reduce from 60 percent stocks to 55 percent stocks." Now if you're managing millions, maybe this is significant, but if you're managing $50,000 or $100,000, just how does this 5 percent change make much difference in your end-of-day investing success?

The answer is that it really doesn't. As a true manager of your investments—a manager of your businesses—you should look at owning a manageable number of specific businesses.

Sure, funds may be a part of how you want to manage part of a portfolio, to relieve yourself of the burden of having to manage it *all* actively. But that should be taken as a deliberate decision, not as a panacea. ("I'm 50 percent stocks and I'm diversified, so I must be doing it right.")

Diversify Across Multiple Dimensions

All this being said, you certainly don't want all your eggs in one basket, no matter how good that basket is. The future for even the safest and strongest bet is uncertain. Business can change, competition can change, a company can lose a CEO or run afoul of accounting rules—there are big rocks out there that can scuttle even the most secure businesses. So some well-conceived diversification does make sense and is the right thing to do.

The best way to think of diversification is multidimensionally, that is, you want to diversify across several dimensions, not just one (e.g., stocks, bonds, cash). Here are some dimensions to consider:

- *Industry.* If it doesn't make sense to put all your eggs in one company basket, it doesn't make more sense to put them all in one or two industry baskets, either. Even solid industries like energy or health care can change, and what is bad for the group almost always hurts all of the players in that group. Even Buffett diversifies across industries—insurance, paint, utilities, transportation, and restaurants. It's best to diversify across at least four to five industries. A good example of industry diversification thinking can be found nightly on CNBC's *Mad Money*, hosted by Jim Cramer, who reviews caller portfolios during a latter segment of the show.

- *Risk profile.* I think it's a good idea to diversify, or segment, investments according to risk profile. This is sort of what some pros get to by diversifying across large cap, mid cap, and small cap (measures for a size of a company). I take the idea a step further by suggesting specifically chosen conservative and more aggressive investments as parts of a complete portfolio. The next habit, Habit 5: Segment, or "Tier," Your Portfolio, describes how a portfolio can be segmented, or "tiered" to diversify by not only risk, but also the amount of time spent managing the different portfolio segments.

- *Time horizon.* Diversifying by time horizon—that is, how long it will take an investment to achieve a return objective—is a variation of the "risk profile" diversification theme—really, it's just another way to look at it. You can think of it as "pay me now" versus "pay me later." You may want some stocks or other investments that pay a current and regular income, balanced with others, perhaps more aggressive growth stocks that promise a larger payback later on. Having some of both—not all "now" stocks, not all "later" ones—is a smart way to diversify.

- *Type of investment: fund versus individual stocks.* As mentioned above, I don't really think the choice of stocks versus bonds versus cash versus commodities and real estate really gets to the point of diversification, although smart investors should probably own all of these or their equivalents (I consider a paid-off mortgage as a form of bond investment; it's a fixed-interest payment that you *save*, rather than collect, and it's even safer than what you buy as a bond). However, in the interest of time and focus on the really important parts of your portfolio, some diversification between funds and individual stocks makes sense. Manage some if it yourself, and let the pros manage some of it for you. You'll get a balance of your ideas and those of others; moreover, you'll find yourself with more time to do a really good job managing what you manage.

Get the Numbers Right

Most time-constrained, resource-constrained investors can and should manage somewhere between five and ten non-overlapping investments. More than that and you may have a hard time with time and focus; fewer than that and you may have too many eggs in one basket. With five investments, you can get enough diversification for the average individual investor. In fact, the aforementioned *Mad Money* diversification reviews on CNBC are done with five investments: Cramer reviews a five-stock portfolio and makes adjustments, suggesting another five-stock portfolio.

Get Into the Habit

- Realize the myths and costs of diversification.
- Avoid overlapping funds and other forms of overdiversification.
- Diversify "deeper" than simple asset allocation: realize that the mix of stocks versus bonds versus cash versus other doesn't go far enough without knowing what's beneath the surface.
- Diversify across multiple "smart" dimensions—industry, risk profile, time horizon and funds vs. individual company stocks.
- Set yourself up to choose and manage between five and ten companies as your primary "focus" investments.

HABIT 5

Segment, or "Tier," Your Portfolio

Warning: Those of you who are faithful readers of my *100 Best Stocks You Can Buy* series will find this habit and its explanation to be fairly familiar to the strategy Scott Bobo and I outline in that book; As a strategy, it can also be considered a valid "habit."

Think of your investment portfolio not as a single entity but as a tiered pyramid of investments, with each tier receiving different amounts of attention and designed to achieve different objectives.

Most readers who've glanced at *100 Best Stocks* might expect it to focus on the virtues of 100 "best" stocks and not to go any further into investing or portfolio strategy. That is not true. Even with the *100 Best Stocks* books, my perspective is that investing by nature goes well beyond simply buying stocks, just like owning an automobile goes far beyond just buying it.

I find that a lot of investors lose the forest in the trees, spending all of their energy trying to find individual stocks or funds without putting enough consideration into their overall investing framework. If they look at the big picture at all, they look at the formulaic covenants of asset allocation (see Habit 4: Find Your Diversification Sweet Spot), a favorite subject of the financial planning and advisory community—as though the difference between 50 percent equities and 60 percent equities makes all the difference in the world. Sure, it might in the world of pension funds and other institutional investments, where a 10 percent adjustment could move millions into or out of a particular asset class and more or less toward safety, but what about a $100,000 portfolio? Does $10,000 more or less in stocks, bonds, or cash make that much difference?

Perhaps not. And of course there's more to that story. Which matters more: That you're 60 percent in equities? Or *which* equities you invest in? Clearly the second is more important than the first. So while asset allocation models make for nice pie charts, we prefer to approach big-picture portfolio constructs differently.

Start with a Portfolio in Mind

You're not a professional investor. You have other things to do with your time, and time is of the essence. You cannot spend forty, fifty, or sixty hours a week glued to a computer screen analyzing your investments.

Further, as an individual investor, you're looking to beat the market. (We reviewed the mathematical rationale of that idea in Habit 2: Know and Use Basic Investing Math.) Not by a ton—20 percent sustained returns simply aren't possible without taking outlandish risks. But perhaps if the market is up by its long-term average of 5 percent in a year, you'd like to achieve 6, perhaps 7 percent without taking excessive risks. On the other hand, if the market is down 20 percent, perhaps you want to cut your losses at 5 or 10 percent. Either way, you're looking to do somewhat better than the market.

Because of time constraints, and owing to your objective to do slightly better than average, I suggest taking a *tiered* approach to your portfolio. The tiers suggested here aren't based on the type of assets; they're based on the amount of activity and attention you want to pay to different parts of your portfolio. It's a strategic portfolio approach you would probably take if you were managing a small business—put most of your focus on the products and customers who might bring the greatest new return to your business; let the rest of your slow steady customer base function as it has for the long term.

I suggest breaking up your portfolio into three *tiers*, or segments. This can be done by setting up specific accounts, or less formally by simply applying the model as a thought process. This thought process and approach is applied consistently and is the "habit."

Let's look at the three segments:

Active Portfolio Segmentation

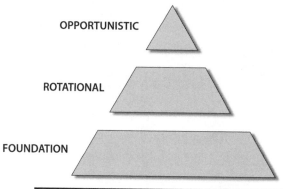

	CLASSIC	CONSERVATIVE	AGGRESSIVE
OPPORTUNISTIC	10-20%	5-10%	20-40%
ROTATIONAL	10-30%	5-10%	10-30%
FOUNDATION	50-80%	80-90%	30-70%

The Foundation Portfolio

In this construct, each investor defines and manages a corner-stone foundation portfolio, which is long-term in nature and requires relatively less active management. Frequently, the foundation portfolio consists of retirement accounts (the paradigmatic long-term investment) and may include your personal residence or other long-lived personal or family assets, such as trusts, collectibles, and so forth. The typical foundation portfolio is invested to achieve at least average market returns through index funds, quality mutual funds, and some income-producing assets like dividend paying stocks or, if conditions warrant it, corporate or public sector bonds held to maturity.

A foundation portfolio may also contain some long-term plays in commodities or real estate to defend against inflation, particularly in such commodities as energy, precious metals, and real estate trusts. The foundation portfolio is largely left alone, although as with all investments it is important to check it at least once in a while to make sure performance—and any professional managers that might be involved, like fund managers—are keeping up with expectations.

The Rotational Portfolio

The second segment, the rotational portfolio, you manage more actively to keep up with changes in business cycles and conditions. It is likely in a set of stocks or funds that might be rotated or remixed occasionally to reflect business conditions or to get a little more offensive or defensive. More than the other portfolios, this portfolio follows the rotation of market preference among different kinds of businesses and business assets. Manage this portfolio to redeploy assets among market or business sectors, between aggressive and defensive business assets, from domestic to international plays, from "large cap" to "small cap" companies, from companies or industries in favor versus out of favor, from stocks to bonds to commodities, and so forth. Sector-specific exchange-traded funds (ETFs) are a favorite component of these portfolios, as are cyclical and commodity-based stocks like gold mining stocks.

Is this about "market timing?" Let's refer to it as "intelligent" or "educated" market timing. Studies have been around for years that tell us that it is impossible to effectively time market moves. It is impossible to catch highs and lows in particular investments, market sectors, or even the market as a whole. Nobody can find exact tops or bottoms. But by watching economic indicators and the pulse of business and the marketplace, you can boost long-term market performance by well-rationalized and timely sector rotation. The key word is timely. The agile and more active investor has enough of a finger on the pulse to see the signs and invest accordingly.

While the idea isn't new, the advent of "low-friction" exchange-traded funds and other index portfolios makes it a lot more practical for the individual investors. What does "low-friction" mean? They trade like a single stock—with all the commission discounts and simplicity of a single stock trade. You don't have to liquidate or acquire a whole basket full of investments on your own to follow a sector. I should note that it's been possible to rotate assets in mutual fund families for years with a single phone call, but most funds in these families are less "pure" plays in their sector, and most families do not cover all sectors.

The Opportunistic Portfolio

The opportunistic portfolio is the most actively traded portion of your total portfolio. The opportunistic portfolio looks for stocks or other investments that seem to be notably under (or over) valued at a particular time. The active investor looks for shorter-term opportunities, perhaps a few days, perhaps a month, perhaps even a year, to wring out short-term gains from undervalued situations.

The opportunistic portfolio also may be used to generate short-term income through covered call option writing (see Habit 22: Pay Yourself). Options are essentially a cash-based risk transfer mechanism whereby a possible, but low-probability investment outcome is exchanged for a less profitable but more certain, and very short-term, cash return scenario. A fee or "premium" is paid in exchange for transferring the opportunity for more aggressive gain to someone else. You collect this fee. Effectively, you as the owner of a stock can convert a growth investment into a shorter-term income investment, paying yourself a dividend for the ownership of the stock by selling an option. Is this risky? Actually, in most situations it is less risky than owning the stock *without* selling an option and converts a long-term investment into a short-term cash generating opportunity.

Curiously, the main objective of the opportunistic portfolio is to generate income, or cash. Most traditional investors look at the long-term, more conservative components of a portfolio to generate income through bonds, dividend-paying stocks, and so forth. In this framework, the short-term opportunistic portfolio actually does the heavy lifting in terms of generating cash income. An active investor might look to trade those stocks with varying degrees of frequency or to sell some options to generate cash. These "swing" trades usually run from a few days to a month or so, and may be day trades if things work out particularly well and fast. However, day trades are not the active investor's goal nor typical practice.

ARE RETIREMENT ACCOUNTS ALWAYS PART OF THE FOUNDATION?

The long-term objectives and nature of retirement accounts suggest normal inclusion as part of the foundation portfolio. Retirement assets can be deployed as part of either the rotational or opportunistic portfolio. In fact, it might make a lot of sense to do so. Why? Because returns generated are tax free, at least until withdrawn. Tax-free returns can compound much faster. Because of the importance of these assets, one should only commit a small portion to an actively managed opportunistic portfolio, but it can be a good way to "juice" the growth of this important asset base.

Learning to Think "Tiers"

Now how do you turn such a segmentation scheme into a useful investing habit?

The first recommendation is to get into the habit, when considering any potential investment, of thinking in tiers. Is the investment best suited as a foundation, a rotational, or an opportunistic investment? Is it most likely to return a short-term gain to help me get to 6 or 7 percent this year, with a more active monitoring? Or is it something I want to simply stuff in my investing mattress for long-term growth and steady or growing payouts, not to attend to or watch on a daily or even a monthly basis?

It makes sense to have some investments both in the foundation and in the opportunistic tiers at any given time, and perhaps some in the rotational tier depending on the size of your portfolio and how actively you wish to manage it.

HOW CAN I USE THE *100 BEST STOCKS?*

Those faithful readers of the sister *100 Best Stocks to Buy* may have already internalized this idea, but here I'll review how you might use the book or a similar list in a tiering scheme:

The *100 Best* list can be used in all tiers, depending on your time horizon and current price relative to value. If a stock on the *100 Best* list takes a nosedive, and feels that nosedive is out of proportion to the real news and near-term prospects of the company, it may be a candidate for the opportunistic portfolio. If the stock makes sense as a long-term holding (as many on the list do) it's a good candidate for the foundation portfolio. Likewise, if you feel that, say, health-care stocks are, as a group, likely to be in favor and are undervalued now, you can pick off the health-care stocks on the *100 Best* list as a rotational portfolio pick. Similarly, if you feel that large-cap dividend-paying stocks will do well, again you can use the *100 Best* list to feed into this hunch.

Get Into the Habit

- Divide your investments into tiers—either by specifically segmenting accounts or simply in your mind (a written list will help you keep track).
- Decide how much of your portfolio should be in each tier, and set expectations for each tier.
- Spend more time managing the more active tiers—the most time devoted to the opportunistic portfolio, less to the rotational, then the least to the foundation portfolio.
- When considering a new investment, think about what tier it should reside in.
- Shop for the best investments for each tier.

Work Hard *and* Work Smart

Contrary to what many think, investing is hard work. So how do you pull it off when it isn't your full-time occupation? Bottom line: Investing should be looked at more like a profession or like raising children. You need to realize that you won't get the desired result immediately or without effort, and you need to set aside the time—and get help where it makes sense—to be successful and to develop your techniques as you go.

Do the Due Diligence

Lots of investors think they can read a book or two (or read a couple of Internet articles), perhaps talk to a broker or adviser briefly, maybe a friend or two, and *voila!*—they know all they need to know. After all, that's all they need to do to play a game of poker—know how the game works, know the order of hands, watch a friend play a hand or two, and join in to learn from the experience.

Such a learning exercise might actually work in poker. Why? Because the game is short, much of it is chance, and you can't lose that much in a given hand. Repeated losses (hopefully with a few victories mixed in) provide valuable experience with minimal loss. Hand by hand you gain experience with likely outcomes and betting tactics. Those experiences are additive, and sooner or later you develop a sense, a reflex, that guides you towards what to do with a given hand.

Investing isn't—or shouldn't be—thought of in the same way. Investing is done over the long haul—and it is hard work. As actor John Houseman once put it: You ". . . make money the old fashioned way. You *earn* it."

When you buy a stock, you are buying a share of a business, an idea that will be expanded in Habit 7: Buy Like You're Buying a Business. It's not a share of a chance event like the draw of a next card or a "flop" of cards. You want to own the business in order to generate a desired return. As such, you should know something about it before you buy it and keep track of it after you buy it. It is a far bigger matter than buying in, playing a hand, and cashing in or folding.

Investing means work. It means doing the same kind of work as before, during, and after the ownership of a business. You must appraise the business and the price (that is, the stock price) to see, given the possible outcomes, whether the price makes sense for the prospects—and the risks—of the business. You should keep up with the business and keep up with change and any indicators of change. And if you sell, you should step back and take inventory of what you learned from the experience, to make you a better investor/business owner the next time around.

Naturally, if you were to set out to buy a business, say, the corner tavern, today, that would require work—understanding how it works, whether or not it is successful, and if so, what makes it successful. Fortunately, as a transaction, the purchase of most stocks is easier than the transaction of buying (or selling) the business. In that transactional respect, buying and selling stocks is less work than buying the business. Next, as an owner, you must keep your fingers on the pulse, although as an owner of stock you have an established management team to do the nuts and bolts for you.

Not to belabor the point, but buying and selling stocks *as an investor* (not trader or speculator) is more like buying and selling companies than like playing poker or participating in other chance games. You need to do your homework. You need to know what you're doing. You need to learn the industry, including the drivers and dynamics of the industry. You need to do the due diligence. You need to keep up. You need to keep working after the purchase. You need to learn from your mistakes so you don't repeat them.

Don't believe for a minute that you can invest without doing at least some work—even if you buy funds or hire a professional adviser to handle some of the work for you.

It Takes Time
Businesses are complex!

The list of complexities is a mile long: raw materials, labor, other inputs, methods, packaging, marketing, and selling, to name a few. Customers, competition, rules, regulatory compliance, taxes, hiring and firing, training, labor relations, and technology, to name a few more. These just scratch the surface of the myriad complexities of buying, owning, and selling a business.

Fortunately, as a stock investor, you've hired someone else (i.e., the directors and management) to take care of the details. You are the owner, but with no real responsibility for running the business. That's a good thing. You're the owner, not the "doer." But to select the right business and be a successful owner, you still need to know something about how the business works.

If you owned the corner tavern, but never set foot in the place because you had managers and employees to "take care of business" for you, it would still require some of your time. Time to make the selection in the first place, time to review the results periodically, time to talk to those in charge of the day-to-day operations. As a stock owner, you do a similar review to buy and another review to examine the results. You probably don't talk to management directly, but you should listen to what they have to say occasionally, at least in the periodic conference calls.

As a stock investor, your "diligence" takes less time than if you owned 100 percent of the business, because a lot of the homework is done for you. Information to analyze the business is readily available and some analysis is already done and available for you, for example, as *Value Line Investment Survey* research reports. Financial "results" statements are readily available in standard formats as quarterly and annual reports.

So the amount of time is less as an investor devoted to a particular stock as opposed to the time put in by the owner of the corner tavern. But you still need to perform many of the same tasks, and you need to set aside the time.

Set Aside the Time

So, *how much* time? That's kind of a tough one. It depends on how much you already know about an industry, about companies in the industry, and about the markets themselves.

There's no real rule of thumb here, as there is in public speaking where most professionals recommend spending an hour of preparation for every minute of speaking time. Really, it's whatever time is required to develop an understanding of what you're doing, make a good choice, and stay on top of the choices made.

When I look to choose a new stock, I might spend at least two to three hours reading and researching everything I can find on a company, assuming some familiarity with the industry it's in. I read the financials. I read research reports including *Value Line.* I read recent news stories and highlights. I study Reuters ("Key Developments" at *www.reuters.com/finance/ stocks/(TICKER SYMBOL)/key-developments* is pretty good for this) as are the finance portals, Yahoo!Finance (*finance. yahoo.com*) and Google Finance (*finance.google.com*). I'll watch the stock and the company for at least a few days to observe price behavior and to see the flavor of what "new" news comes forth. I may do this for weeks.

Once I buy, and really, with my entire "active" portfolio and especially my "opportunistic" plays (see Habit 5: Segment, or "Tier," Your Portfolio) I watch them at least daily through my financial portal. I set the portal so that news stories related to my holdings are displayed on the news item list. I monitor earnings reports as they come across, and I listen to conference calls when they happen. I probably spend at least half an hour a day watching, and more time—maybe an hour or more, at least once a week—catching up. More time is spent reading business and economic articles as they come through to get a better sense of where the economy and industry in general are headed. This may average another half-hour a day, with considerable variation around that figure depending on what's going on.

That's my model. Yours will vary according to needs, time available, and media available, but you should put a routine in place and set aside the time.

Get Help When You Need It

To use a professional adviser or not to use a professional adviser? That is the question almost all individual investors ask themselves at one time or another.

Individual investors are independent, self-starting, self-driven folks largely capable of accepting responsibility for their own decisions and actions. That's good, and I assume that if you're reading this, you have at least some of that character. However, the world isn't so simple, and your time isn't so plentiful, and maybe business and investing stuff just isn't your cup of tea, anyway. You don't want to throw everything over the wall to a professional adviser (and pay the fees and lose control and all that), but you may want some help from time to time.

Just remember this—you, you only, and ultimately you are responsible for your own finances, just like a pilot flying an airplane is ultimately responsible for what happens to that airplane and its passengers. You are in charge. That's true whether or not you have someone else, like a broker or professional adviser, helping you out. You're still the boss.

You can (and should) think of an adviser as more like a co-pilot, navigator, or air traffic controller—who will give you information and suggestions and help you interpret the information and remind you of the rules when necessary—but ultimately you're in charge.

Financial advisers come in many forms, and I won't go into the details here. What's important is to realize that no matter how much you outsource, you're still at the helm. You need to develop a good, two-way relationship with the adviser, one in which he can bring value and help you bring value to the investment decisions and investment strategy. He shouldn't tell you what to do, but he shouldn't just be the "yes man" for everything you want to do. A lively, point-counterpoint discussion of any financial move with an adviser is healthy; two heads are better than one. Remember, if two people think the exact same way, you don't need one of them.

Don't be snowed by fancy terminology and concepts. Investing is a complex subject, but if the explanation sounds more complex than the task itself, look out below. Find an adviser who speaks your language, that is, plain English. Smart, experienced people make things simple, not complex, for others.

Also be clear what you want and what you expect from an adviser. If you don't spell out your expectations, he'll give you the "standard" product, and it may be the same standard product he gave his last client. Say that you want help constructing your portfolio and learning about, say, the tech and health care sectors, which you don't know enough about. Ask him to help you understand the headlines and what's important about them for the banking industry. And so forth.

And of course, as Bernard Madoff showed us—make sure you understand what he's doing, if he's managing anything on your behalf. There is nothing worse than thinking everything is okay, when in fact it's completely off in the weeds.

Bottom line, an investment adviser should be a great partner, someone you'd hire into your business if you were trying to create a partnership in the investing business. Look for common sense; look for the adviser to help you most with the things you're least comfortable with. Learn what he does (and have done) with other clients; if it sounds too good to be true, it probably is.

Here's another bottom line: your adviser should make you sleep better at night. If you're waking up at 3 A.M. thinking about your investments, that's bad. If you're waking up at 3 A.M. thinking about your adviser, that's worse. In both cases, they're too risky for you.

Use Funds Where It Makes Sense

Smart business owners don't try to do everything themselves. Typically, at the outset, they decide what they can do, and should do, given their skill sets, time, and what's on their plate to manage. Then they delegate the rest to others, while of course (and as just discussed) keeping tabs on those others, what they do, and how well they do it.

You may or may not choose a personal professional investment adviser to help you along, and to supply another professional opinion in the construction of your investment portfolio—as just discussed above. Another way to get some help is to buy and hold funds, rather than individual stocks, in your portfolio.

There are two types of funds. The first is actively managed funds, where a professional manager essentially makes your stock picks for you based on his own analysis and within the confines of a fund's declared investment style. Most, but not all, "mutual" funds are of this type.

The second is passively managed funds, constructed and rather vigorously maintained around a predefined index, a basket of companies aligned to a particular stock index, geography, industry, or a more specific investing objective, for instance, "dividend" stocks or "wind energy" companies.

By buying a fund, you're essentially leaving the driving to someone else, either the "active" fund manager or the entity that constructs and maintains the index in the case of passive funds. By delegating some part of your portfolio—often the *foundation* portfolio (see Habit 5)—to someone else, you can devote more of your time to the specific companies you choose to own and manage.

You should manage your fund investments much as you manage your stock investments—choose carefully and with a rationale, and watch what happens. By owning these managed investments, you'll probably spend less time on them and take less risk with them, while at the same time earning smaller rewards. The issue is really time, expertise, and diversification—by buying funds you gain some of all three. See Habit 9: Appraise Funds Realistically.

Turn It All Into a Routine

By now, you probably saw this coming. Like working a job, raising kids, or owning the corner tavern, soon the management of your investment portfolio will become a matter of routine. You'll figure out a regular schedule, a regular set of resources, and a regular set of delivery mechanisms (printed media, Internet, tablet, smartphone, etc.) that bring the greatest efficiency, that is, the most knowledge for the time and money invested.

The important part is to make it a routine. For the most part, especially in today's dynamic business and investing climate, you can't simply buy an investment and forget about it. You can't do a superficial analysis of a company "destined to make money" forever and lock it away without checking things once in a while. Eastman Kodak investors know what I'm talking about.

Get Into the Habit

- Do the homework, just as if you're buying and owning the whole business.
- Set aside the time to do it right, both initially and ongoing.
- Get help where you need it—in the form of professional advisers and in the form of fund investments.
- Turn it into a routine.

PART II

APPRAISE FOR SUCCESS: FINDING YOUR VERY BEST INVESTMENTS

Over time you'll perform four tasks as an investor. First, you'll learn about investments, and you'll learn about investing if you're new to the game. Then, you'll buy, you'll own, and you'll sell your chosen investments. In Part I, you've acquired some of the basics. In Part II, it's time to shop—and if everything checks out, to buy!

The twelve habits presented in Part II will help you make the very best "buy" decisions. You'll learn to buy stocks and other investments in much the same way you'd think about buying an entire business.

HABIT 7

Buy Like You're Buying a Business

You've seen or heard this one before. If you have attentively read Habit 6: Work Hard *and* Work Smart and most of the other five habits in Part I, you've probably already gotten the idea.

But it bears repeating. Why? Because it is arguably the most important habit you can possibly adopt. It's like Christ to a Christian or measuring to a carpenter. It is the most central, the most sacred core of the investing enterprise, and without it you may well end up with nothing—or worse.

When you're investing, you're buying a business.

When you become an investor, you become a businessperson. A businessperson invests money—*capital*—into a business for no other reason than to produce a return. Not for bragging rights, not for the cocktail party value of saying, "I made a killing on a few shares of Facebook the other day." Not for ego or for the thrills and frills. But inevitably and always for the sake of producing a solid return on the hard-earned capital invested.

So, you should approach it that way.

It is a core value of the successful investor.

The Main Idea

By its very nature, my discussion of Habit 7 will be shorter and simpler than most of the others you'll read. Why? Because it's really a mentality and thought process, not a method or a checklist.

Buying shares in a company should be undertaken as though you're buying the whole business, 100 percent of it, to become its sole owner. For most of us, all we can afford is a few shares, a tiny percentage of the company. That doesn't matter—you should approach the decision and ongoing management as though you're buying the whole thing, and pretend that you're actually doing that.

Alternative Approaches Don't Count

Although the markets are full of investors and "players" who don't do it this way, if you stick to the notion of buying good businesses—and learn to separate good businesses from the rest—you'll be successful. Those players may win some hands in the short run and may come away with some stories to tell, but they won't necessarily invest in good businesses. Thus, in the long run, most are setting themselves up to fail.

Sometimes the best way to explain what something *is* is to explain what it *isn't*. I'll use that tactic here.

- *Momentum investing.* Company XYZ is on the move. Going up steadily. A buck or two every day. Time to jump on the bandwagon, right? Buy what is going up. In fact, Warren Buffett remarked that the stupidest reason to buy a stock is because it is going up. While that can help validate that something is a good idea, it probably means that you're paying too much, and that your "margin of safety" (see Habit 18: Buy with a Margin of Safety) is compromised. Although you should check the price along the way (see Habit 19: Buy Smart—When You Decide to Buy) you should never *start* the process with the stock price.

- *Technical investing.* "Buy when the stock rises beyond its 50-day or 200-day moving average, on strengthening volume, and when its moving average convergence-divergence indicator (MACD) rises above the signal line." What's going on here? Whoever is recommending this approach is acting based on stock price behavior, which has little to nothing to do with the business represented by the stock. True, technical analysis attempts to quantify and depict the collective behavior of *all* investors and traders into a repeatable and actionable pattern and set of signals, but is it buying a business? Most technical traders don't even know what the business *is* behind the stock they are buying.

- *Buy the industry.* "Buy XYZ Corp because it's in the health-care industry, and health care has nowhere to go but up." Although this comes closer to addressing the fundamentals of a business, because a business is part of an industry, it still stops short of buying a business. You wouldn't buy just any corner tavern in order to get into the restaurant industry, right? Such "can't miss" industry investing comes and goes—dot.com, homebuilding, energy, semiconductors, and others all have had their heyday. You know the rest of the story.

- *Stock-tip investing.* "A buddy of mine told me about Rare Earth Resources. He read an article about it online, and it's gotta rise because of China demand—and they aren't making any more of the stuff." Might be a good idea and a good rationale for further investigation. But is it a good business? Maybe—but probably not. Stocks should be something you want to *buy*, not things that are sold to you by others.

- *Peer-pressure investing.* "Everyone owns XYZ, and all the analysts have rated it a 'buy.'" Don't feel pressured to own something because everyone else does. The fact that everyone is on the bandwagon doesn't make it a good investment.
- *Pure trading.* Buying and selling to make short-term profits can work, and it is commonly successful for the short-term dealer or market player. But again, such traders seldom base decisions on the business, but rather simply on the stock price. Does this qualify as investing? No!

Buy Businesses, Not Just Good Ideas

Is Facebook a good investment? Or is it just a good idea? That's the sort of decision that confronted many investors in May 2012, and one that you must undertake nearly every time you consider or hear about a new investment.

At one time or another all of us have been taken by fantastic, can't-miss ideas that are made to look great by the people pushing them. Others *seem* great from our own personal experiences.

The investing world is littered with their carcasses, as most of you know who were around for the 1999–2001 "dot.com" investing boom. These ideas looked great. Use the Internet to order your groceries and distribute them from a central warehouse to avoid the costs of staffing, stocking, and maintaining large neighborhood supermarkets. Lots of cost savings, plus everybody was learning to do everything on the Internet, right?

But the idea—and its largest suitor, Webvan Group, Inc.—fell flat on its face after a short two-year ride. Why? The concept required huge capital investments in warehouses and delivery mechanisms. It was hard to stock every food item required. Moreover, it was hard for a lot of customers to abandon the idea of checking the tomatoes in person to see if they were fresh. Another thing that got in the way was the need to be home to accept the delivery—which was usually not an option for people busy enough to want the service in the first place.

So what seemed like a great and very timely *idea* wasn't ready to become a *business*. The *fundamentals* weren't right, and the *intangibles* weren't right. As a result, Webvan failed quickly, as did many other web-based enterprises originally thought to be (or sold to be) sure things for investors.

Deciding whether something really passes the "smell test" of a good business—as opposed to a good idea—is one of the first and most important tasks you can perform as an investor. Is Facebook a good business or just a great idea? Yes! It *must* be a great idea—over a billion people have signed up. Your job as an investor is to try to figure out if it's a good business, and one worth the approximately $100 billion in market value price tag in the public offering.

Most of the rest of the habits in Part II cover the sort of fundamentals and intangibles that will help you distinguish between a good *business* and (just) a good idea.

Get Into the Habit

- Think of buying a stock like you're buying 100 percent of the business.
- Always think about the business, *and then* look at the price.
- Don't fall for something just because it sounds like a good idea.

HABIT 8

Buy What You Understand, Understand What You Buy

It won't be hard to recognize this habit as a continuation of Habit 7: Buy Like You're Buying a Business. In Habit 7 I stressed the importance of treating any investment in any company as though you were buying the entire business and planned to own the business for yourself, even if you were just buying a few shares of it. Remember that you are buying a *company*, not a stock.

Not surprisingly, that entails developing a keen understanding of the business, just as you would do if you were considering buying the corner tavern or restaurant. True, you're hiring professionals—the directors and managers employed by the company—to manage it for you on a day-to-day basis. But that doesn't excuse you from being knowledgeable or involved as an owner.

The habit being described here is the use of a combination of life experience, skills, learning, and just plain looking around to really grasp a business and understand its underlying fundamentals and what makes it tick.

The corollary habit—and perhaps the one that is most important and most often forgotten: if you *don't* understand a business, don't buy it.

Go with What You Know—and What You Can Find Out

Consider the description given for the glamorous and popular $40 billion technology solutions provider VMware (ticker symbol VMW). Front and center on Google Finance, it goes like this:

> *VMware, Inc. is a provider of virtualization and virtualization-based cloud infrastructure solutions. The Company's suite of virtualization solutions addresses a range of information technology (IT) issues that include facilitating access to cloud computing capacity, business continuity, software lifecycle management, and corporate end user computing device management.*

Do you know what this means? What the heck *is* virtualization, anyway? What's the product? Who needs it and why? How does a company make money off of it?

Would you buy this company? *Should* you buy this company?

I can't say that you should or shouldn't. But I can say this: you'd better understand a lot about virtualization and the news and nuances about cloud computing, especially before paying some fifty times earnings (as many before you have) to buy this company. Translation: you *probably* shouldn't buy this company.

I can tell you something else: Warren Buffett and many other successful investors wouldn't touch this issue with a ten-foot pole.

Why? Simple. They just don't understand the business. It's too hard to figure out whether this company has a competitive advantage or any other market advantage, a production cost advantage, a customer loyalty advantage, or any other *sustainable* advantage to make it a solid future bet. It's too hard to read what drives marketplace—or financial—success. It's too hard to keep up with change. Wouldn't it simply be easier to buy a *relatively* simpler company that sells hamburgers and milk shakes by the billions, like McDonald's?

Yes it would, for most people. But some of you with a technology background may actually understand this stuff. And some of you who don't quite have that background but are willing to study the industry and get tuned in to the latest trends and developments. You may be "wired in" to the latest news and have smart friends who work in the industry and can explain the industry and its latest developments to you. If you have the aptitude, inclination, *and* the connections to the latest industry trends, then you *might* learn enough to be able invest in this business.

Too many investors these days do not go far enough to learn and understand their business. Something *sounds* like a good idea, so they take the plunge with no hope of really understanding what they're buying. Such plays sometimes work out due to luck, but they stop well short of being a sustainable investing methodology.

THE WEBSITE TEST

When considering an investment, I recommend a tour through a company's website to get more familiar with the company, what it does, what its products are, and how it conveys what it does to the outside world. If you understand what you see on the site and can easily explain it in your own words to someone else, you're getting there.

If you can visualize yourself as the webmaster responsible for creating the website and think you could have done just as good a job as the real webmaster, then you probably understand the business. On the other hand, If you conclude that "there's no way in hell" that you could have developed, or could even amend, a company's website, your money probably doesn't belong there.

In Sight Can Be Insight

Two of the most widely followed investment "gurus" of our age, Peter Lynch and Warren Buffett, have stressed the idea of buying businesses you know about and understand. This idea naturally follows the entrepreneurial idea of buying stocks as if you were buying a business; if you didn't understand the business, would you be comfortable buying it?

Peter Lynch, former manager of the enormous Fidelity Magellan fund and author of the well-known 1989 bestseller *One Up on Wall Street*, gave us the original notion of buying what you know. He suggests that the best investment ideas are those you see—and can learn about and keep track of—in daily life, on the street, on the job, in the mall, in your home. A company such as Starbucks makes sense to Lynch because you can readily see the value proposition and how it extends beyond coffee. You can follow customer response and business activity at least in part just by hanging around your own neighborhood edition.

And I hardly need mention the subject of iPods, iPads, and their use—how they've turned Apple into the most valuable company in the world—and how plainly visible their success has been.

With his investments Buffett has famously stuck with businesses that are easy to understand—paint, carpet, electric utilities (although he deals with the fantastically complicated businesses of casualty insurance and re-insurance in his core Berkshire Hathaway business). He has shunned technology investments because he doesn't understand them, and more than likely, because their value and consumer preference shifts too fast for him to keep up.

Both approaches make sense, and especially in hindsight, they would have kept us further from trouble in the 2008–2009 crash. Many, many investors didn't understand financial firms as well as they should have; the preponderance of evidence suggests that those financial firms didn't even understand themselves!

Clearly, you won't understand everything about the businesses you invest in—there's a lot of complexity and detail even behind the cooking and serving of hamburgers at McDonald's! Further, a sizeable amount of good knowledge is confidential so you likely won't ever get your hands on it. So you need to go with what you know and realize that a lot of the devil is in the details. When you analyze a company, if you can say, "The more you know, the better," instead of, "The more you know, the more you don't know," you'll be better off.

Don't Miss Out on the Big Picture

Popular expressions abound concerning the importance of the big picture when you make any sort of decision. The phrase "Don't lose the forest in the trees" enjoys no finer hour than when tied to the subject of investing.

Technologies and consumer tastes change. If you doubt that for a minute, simply think of Eastman Kodak and digital photography or the evolving and still uncertain transition from the PC to the tablet. Such changes affect even the best businesses. Add to this the idea of change brought on by demographic trends (the aging of the population, for instance) and changes in law and policy (toward "green," toward universal healthcare, toward lower or higher interest rates, for instance) and you end up with a heck of a lot of change and "big picture" influences that can affect your stock picks.

Many investors employ sector analysis as a starting point. Where sector analysis makes sense is in capturing and correctly assessing the larger trends in that sector or industry. The sector thus becomes the arena in which to appraise those trends, often by reading sector analyses published in the media or in trade publications in that sector. You can, and should, learn about the construction industry or health-care industry before investing in a company in that industry.

Once you understand the sector trends, a portfolio selection of a company, or companies, in that sector can make more sense. A good example is PC makers Hewlett-Packard (a former *100 Best Stocks* choice) and Dell (not a choice, although, for different reasons, Dell appears on the *100 Best Aggressive Stocks 2012* list).

Does the Company Have the Right Stuff?

Not surprisingly, part of the process of understanding a business is to understand what drives success. Most people believe that means developing a thorough understanding of the financials. That isn't off the mark, but it is incomplete, as something must also drive the financials. Financials are a lagging indicator of success; what I'll later refer to as "intangibles," such as brand, market position, and management, are leading indicators of the financials and thus are leading indicators for the overall business.

As will be laid out in more detail in the rest of Part II, the prudent investor should understand everything possible about what drives customer satisfaction, customer purchase, sales and revenues, costs, and profits for the company.

Get Into the Habit

- Make sure you understand a company you're thinking about owning.
- Be able to state the company's business in a simple few statements to— say—a family member.
- Make sure you have the background and the connections to find out what you need to know about a company.
- If you don't understand it, don't buy it. Move on. There are plenty of companies out there.

HABIT 9

Appraise Funds Realistically

Throughout habits 4 through 8 we've covered the idea of diversification, portfolio segmentation, working smart, and investing in what you know. One of the best ways to be true to these habits is to use *funds* as an investment tool.

Funds can save you time and round out your portfolio to cover areas you're less familiar with, while adding diversification and an element of safety. But funds are not an "end"— they are a means to an end and should be used wisely and discretely to accomplish specific objectives. They shouldn't be used just because they're there, because an adviser recommends them, or because all of your friends have them. More importantly, don't assume that just because it's a fund it's a good investment. That said, I recognize that especially in certain company-sponsored retirement arrangements such as 401(k) plans, funds are the only choice.

Habit 9 is about making smart use of funds. It doesn't mandate whether to use them or not, but instead is designed to get you in the habit of making good decisions about them.

Topics covered include the types of funds available, costs and benefits of funds, and how to evaluate them objectively.

What are "Funds?"

Funds are groups of securities packaged up into a single security, which you can buy and sell. Think of funds as packaged investments. Packaged investments, like packaged consumer products, make it easier for you to buy, and in this case sell, something. They are produced and marketed by a single producer, have a defined list of contents, a brand or label under which they are sold, in some cases a distribution channel (like your financial adviser)—and importantly, there is a cost associated with providing the package.

As packaged investments, you can also consider them as *managed* investments. At some level, what's included in the package is managed for you by a professional fund manager or index creator whom you implicitly hire to do this work for you. As such, by buying funds you are getting some professional help.

For our purposes, there are two types of funds:

1. *Mutual funds.* Mutual funds are managed investments, usually brought to market as fund families by specialized fund advisers like T. Rowe Price, Putnam, and similar specialized fund managers. Many brokerages, such as Charles Schwab and Merrill Lynch, also offer traditional mutual funds. Mutual funds are typically *actively* managed—that is, there is a human at the controls making buy and sell decisions—although more recently some are simply tied to indexes. When you buy a share of a mutual fund, the money is used directly to buy more securities for the portfolio, and you automatically own a portion of the portfolio proportionate to

your share of the ownership in the fund. When you buy and sell funds, you typically deal with the fund manager directly; funds are not traded on stock exchanges. Funds charge for their services, usually a management fee and a marketing fee (known rather enigmatically as a "12-b-1 fee"), which is assessed against the value of the underlying investment pool (and thus, your shares) each year.

2. *Exchange-traded funds.* ETFs are—well—as the name implies, traded on exchanges, mainly the "Arca" electronic trading branch of the New York Stock Exchange. For reasons that will become clearer below, ETFs are the new hot thing in the fund space. Rather than being "actively" determined by a human fund manager, the contents of an ETF "package" are determined by an index. In the early days, these indexes were confined to the familiar major market indexes. A proliferation of interest in ETFs has led to a proliferation of indexes (or perhaps the other way around)—for, say, wind energy providers or agricultural commodity producers. The contents of the ETF are mapped to the contents and proportions of the index. Outstanding shares trade back and forth between investors, as with individual stocks— these funds are as easy and cheap for you to buy and sell as individual stocks. Administrative costs are assessed and removed from the portfolio, but the simplicity, lack of a human fund manager, and reduced marketing costs (i.e., no commissions) mean that total costs can be much lower than their mutual fund counterparts.

The Basics: Individual Stocks Versus Funds

Packaged investments are offered by intermediaries, which can be investment companies with professional managers choosing specific investments and otherwise looking after the portfolio. They can also be indexes, where groups of like stocks are accumulated into an index according to some sort of generally fixed formula. Most mutual funds are professionally managed, and most ETFs are tied to indexes, but there are exceptions on both sides. Either way, by buying into one of these intermediaries, you're giving up picking individual investments in favor of a packaged and sometimes professionally managed approach.

Of course, like any value proposition, you're giving up something in the interest of gaining something else. The "something else" you're trying to gain by using the packaged approach is usually a combination of the following:

- *Time*—you don't have the time to research and manage individual stocks for 100 percent of your portfolio.
- *Expertise*—in the case of managed funds, you're getting a trained, experienced, investment professional. You may want to hire others to do the work to take the emotion out of investing decisions.
- *Diversification*—by definition, both managed and index funds spread your investments so that you don't have too much wrapped up in a single company; this is generally good unless they diversify away any chance of outperforming the markets (see Habit 4). Funds and ETFs also allow you to play in markets otherwise difficult to play in for lack of knowledge or time (e.g., China growth stocks, alternative energy, etc.).
- *Convenience*—it takes work to build and manage an investment portfolio. With funds you can move in and out of the markets with a single transaction.

Of course, with any value proposition comes a downside, and the downsides of fund and index investing are often underappreciated by investors:

- *Fees and costs*—Not surprisingly, funds, and especially mutual funds, charge money for the packaging and services they provide. Actively managed funds can take a half percent to more than 2 percent of your asset value each year, whether they do well or not. If you understand compounding math (see Habit 2: Know and Use Basic Investing Math), you know that the difference between a 5 percent return and a 3 percent return net of fees over time is huge. Index funds and ETFs are better in this regard, usually charging 0.10 to 0.50 percent, but it still puts a drag on your investing outcomes.
- *Tax efficiency*—When ordinary mutual funds sell shares, any gains flow through to you (unless you hold them in a tax-free or tax-deferred retirement account). You cannot control when this happens, and many "active" funds may roll their portfolios frequently, producing adverse tax consequences. Also, you need to watch when you enter the fund—you should buy in *after* capital gains are paid out, not before, or else effectively you'll be paying taxes on someone else's gains. Index funds and ETFs are far less likely to produce "unwanted" gains, for they tie their investments to the indexes, which don't change much in composition, and thus don't create much buying and selling within the fund.
- *Control*—With funds of any sort, you lose control, and few things are more painful than having someone else lose your money for you. Particularly with managed funds, you really don't know what they're doing with

your money except in hindsight, as most disclose their complete holdings only quarterly.

- *Tendency toward mediocrity*—One of the biggest criticisms of funds over time is the tendency for managers to follow each other and to follow standard business-school investing and risk-management formulas. The result: you tend to get in practice a herd instinct, known in the trade as an "institutional imperative." You can see this in many funds—pick almost any fund and the top ten holdings are GE, Microsoft, ExxonMobil—you get the idea. Worse—and this is a biggie—when you buy a fund and especially an index fund, you're getting all the companies in the industry—the mediocre players, the weak hands—not just the best ones.

So, as a "habit," you should mainly use funds when you don't have the time or confidence to invest. Or you can use funds to get some exposure to an industry or a segment of the market otherwise difficult to access or outside your expertise. Use funds to round out a portfolio or build a foundation or rotational portfolio (See Habit 5: Segment, or "Tier," Your Portfolio), and to save yourself the time and bandwidth to focus more closely on other more "opportunistic" investments.

The Basics: Comparing Mutual Funds and ETFs

Exchange-traded funds have grown from the first one in 1993 and about 100 available in 2001 to more than 1,300 available today. So what the heck is so good about them, and how do they compare to traditional mutual funds?

Among less significant others, there are two core advantages of ETFs:

1. *Transparency*—When you buy a fund, you would like to know what's in that fund, that is, what's in the package. Not that you have to know everything about every security in the fund, but you'd like to see at least in a general sense what the fund owns and how much of it. ETFs offer that transparency. You can see the fund holdings every night, not just on a printed quarterly statement. An adjunct to this notion of transparency: Most ETFs (all but thirty-four *actively managed* funds, in fact) are constructed around an established index. The fund buys and sells stocks almost exactly according to the index. So you can see what's going on, and don't have a fund manager making decisions you don't know about or may not approve of.

2. *Cost*—Because they follow indexes, and because they trade like stocks (simpler) and because the investing public was tired of paying big bucks for investment managers who couldn't even match the performance of major stock market indexes like the S&P 500 Index, ETFs came to being with a low-cost model. Fees for equity ETFs average about 0.6 percent—and many are much lower—in contrast to something north of 1 percent for traditional mutual funds (it was further north of 1 percent than it is now—thanks of course to the presence and competition from ETFs). Further, it is much easier to buy and sell ETFs. Yes, you'll have to pay a brokerage commission, which might be $10 or less at an online broker, but it is much easier to get in, to get out, and to change your fund preferences.

So, what are the downsides? ETF shortcomings include:

- *Frequent overdiversification*—ETFs, by nature, buy baskets of securities. Such diversification can be a good thing, because it insulates you from the problems an individual company might get unlucky enough to fall into. Oil giant BP and its 2010 Gulf of Mexico disaster is a great example. The energy industry may have a great long-term future, but here's a company that lost as much as half its value because of one incident. Buying an energy ETF with many large multinational producers would insulate you from this threat. But if that ETF has every single producer in its portfolio, you know you're getting the bad and the ugly with the good. You know at the outset that you won't—can't—beat the returns of that sector, because you own the sector, and you're getting hit with expenses during that ownership. So unless you intend to track a complete index like the S&P 500, we tend to shy away from funds that have too many— say, more than 100—stocks. Most ETFs range from 20 to more than 1,800 holdings.

- *Still, a middleman*—There is cost, and even if low at 0.20, 0.30, maybe 0.50 percent, that cost is deducted from your investment continuously. There is also something called "tracking error" which arises when the middleman can't adjust the portfolio composition to precisely reflect the index. So you might not get quite the returns you had in mind.

- *Indexes can be complex*—ETFs, and their indexes, are financial "products." And we all know that the past decade has been one of so-called "financial engineering" and some of those engineered products have been, well, over-engineered. So some indexes can have very complex and hard-to-understand selection and weighting schemes, which you should take the time to understand before committing lots of cash. (Incidentally, you can usually get to a pretty good description of an underlying index just by entering its name into a search engine.)

THE 100 BEST ETFS YOU CAN BUY 2012

To get a closer look at the ETF space and to learn about some good funds and how to evaluate funds, I recommend, of course, my own book *The 100 Best ETFs You Can Buy 2012* (coauthored with Scott Bobo), with the caveat that it might be a little out of date by the time you read this. ETFs don't change that much, and again, the thought process is what's really important.

Evaluating Funds

In a relatively short space, I've shared some thought and practical insight about the fund world; insight that I believe necessary to make intelligent choices about using funds (mutual funds and ETFs) in the first place. But in the course of your investing, you'll have to make decisions not only about whether to use funds in the first place, but which funds to use.

The analysis of a given fund is complex, and often, especially with mutual funds, you must get through the marketing and sales "message" to see what you're really buying and what it really costs. That isn't always easy (I chuckle when a fund company bases the advertised virtues of its funds *solely* on past performance—we're going forward in time, not backward!) Here is a simplified four-step approach to evaluating a fund that should become "habit" for fund investors:

- *Congruence with your investing objectives.* Does a fund do what you're really trying to do? Suppose you want to invest in emerging Asian economies. You check out a bunch of international funds, only to find most of their holdings to be in Canada, England, France, and Germany. There are plenty of funds out there—almost 10,000 at last count—so it makes sense to shop until you find what you want. That also requires that you . . .

- *Check what's under the hood.* Use online resources. I've found Fidelity to be best (*www.fidelity.com*) but fund websites can also help to see what the fund actually owns. How many stocks or other securities, and *which* stocks and or other securities, are inside the package? Are the securities ones you'd want to own yourself? Would you want to own the individual securities yourself? If the answer isn't "yes," you probably shouldn't own the fund.

- *Performance.* Although, as they say in the industry, "past performance doesn't guarantee future returns," it's probably worth at least a brief tour of the past to see if the fund has held its own at all against the major market indexes. After all, the reason to buy any fund—or any stock or group of stocks—in the first place is to beat (even slightly) the market rate of return. If you can't do that, you might as well invest 100 percent in an index ETF (some are under 0.10 percent fees) and head for the mall or golf course.

- *Cost.* Like any product you would buy (and if you don't think of funds as a product you're on the wrong track) it should be worth the money—the fees and expenses— that you pay for it. Understand those fees and expenses, and understand what you're getting for it.

Get Into the Habit

- Understand the advantages of funds vs. individual stocks, know where funds may better meet your needs, and act accordingly. Map out a *strategy* for using funds in your portfolio—e.g., to achieve international diversification, exposure to commodities, exposure to small-cap stocks, etc.

- Know how traditional mutual funds and ETFs compare; be prepared to shop the assortment of mutual funds and ETFs to fill the gaps in your portfolio.

- Evaluate funds by objective congruence, holdings, performance, and cost. Test the fund to see if it really does what it says it does, and what *you* want it to do.

- Avoid buying overlapping funds—too much diversification.

- Don't assume that just because the fund comes from a famous Wall Street firm and is wrapped up in a nice package, that it is right for you. It is like any other product and should be evaluated accordingly.

HABIT 10

Value Thy Fundamentals

All businesses have fundamentals. *Fundamentals* are basic, measurable facts about a business that help tell insiders (i.e., management) and outsiders (i.e., investors) how things are going. Fundamentals are to a business what the instruments in an airplane cockpit are to an airplane—airspeed, altitude, attitude, fuel consumption, fuel in the tank, and direction being the most important. Any deviance from the norm in any fundamental signals a need for corrective action. If all fundamentals are falling apart at once, you're in a whole lot of trouble.

Most business fundamentals come forth as financial, or dollar-denominated numbers. Some compare other measurable operational numbers to something financial—for example, sales per square foot in the retail industry. Fundamentals can be represented in dollars (e.g., inventories) or percentages of dollars (profit margin) or ratios (sales per employee).

Your job, as you set out to acquire a business and to own it, is to understand the financials and what drives the company's success. Your job, as a current or future business owner, is to decide:

- Are the financials what they should be?
- Are they getting better or worse?
- Would you want to own the business?

What are "Strategic" Fundamentals?

Business fundamentals can measure anything about a business, but usually measure something about assets, liabilities, revenues or expenses in the business, or the relationship among more than one of these. For example sales per square foot is an efficiency measure measuring the amount of revenue per unit of floor space, an asset.

The hundreds of things you could possibly measure would take a huge amount of time, and most, such as sales per delivery truck owned, would be meaningless. For many it would be hard for you to decide what was "good" or "bad." Here's where being an investor is better than a manager directly involved in the business—you don't have to look at much, just a few key *strategic* fundamentals to judge a company's performance by.

Why Are Fundamentals Important?

Strategic fundamentals can tell you if the business is doing well, if it is on track, and even more importantly, can signal whether things are getting better or worse.

Financial statements provide a record of a company's performance, that is, how much it sold, what it cost to produce those sales, what it owns as assets to conduct the business, and what it owes to others. Almost all financials look to the past.

They reflect past performance, although some, like long-term debt, suggest something about future performance.

The sharp business manager and investor alike understand the past and the measurements of that past. A business with a poor past or current performance is suspect from the beginning, but even a superb performance in the past doesn't guarantee future success (I'll cite again the Eastman Kodak example).

So financial fundamentals—even the most strategic ones—are at best only part of the story. One must also look at the *intangibles*, the characteristics of the firm in regard to its marketplace, its management, sales channels, and so forth, to get a complete picture (as we will in Habits 12–15). Tomorrow's intangibles become yesterday's financials.

At the end of the day, financial fundamentals reveal the strength of two key intangibles:

1. How strong the company is in its marketplace
2. How effectively management converts that strength into profits

Savvy investors get into the habit of reading both of these qualities.

GETTING REAL: A FEW WORDS ABOUT THE "MAGIC" OF ACCOUNTING

Accounting is the language and process of measuring business activity. Most business fundamentals arise from accounting processes.

Contrary to public perception, accounting for business assets and activity is not always a precise science. In fact, there can be quite a bit of art involved in accounting, especially for business assets and business income. As a result, reading financial statements can become one of those "let the buyer beware" exercises.

Why? Because, while the purchase *price* for most "physical" assets is known, the *value* of those assets over time is a subjective calculation. There are many assets, such as intellectual property, that elude precise evaluation altogether. How much is a patent worth? How much is an acquired business worth? Just like a stock you buy, you know what you paid for it, but how much is it really worth in terms of future returns to the acquiring company? It's a fairly subjective number.

Likewise, reported net income can also be somewhat subjective. How much depreciation expense was taken against assets and thus against income? How much "expense" was taken to write down intangible assets such as patents and other intellectual property? How much "restructuring" expense was incurred? The rules give the accountants and corporate management considerable flexibility to "manage" reported earnings as well as asset values: what you see may not always be what you get.

The bottom line is this: while assets and income probably have some subjectivity in their valuation, debts are quite real, and so is cash. Debts must be paid sooner or later; there is no subjectivity or "art" to their valuation. Likewise, cash is cash, the stuff in the proverbial drawer, and is a take-it-or-leave-it, like-it-or-not fact of life or death for a business.

Thus we look at assets and income as important measures of business activity but know that there's some subjectivity in those measures. At the same time, we look at debts, cash, and cash flow in and out of the business as absolute; neither cash nor debts lie. So we hang our valuation hats on cash and debt where we can.

There is more about this in Habit 11: Look for Cash in All the Right Places.

Habitual Strategic Fundamentals

An "acid test" is a quick indicator, or measure, of a chemical reaction or process. You may choose to develop your own list of "acid tests" of the strategic fundamentals of a company. These tests should be applied before buying and while owning the company.

Profit Margins—Healthy, Better, or Worse?

I like profitable companies; who doesn't? But what really counts is the size of the margin and especially the growth. If a company has a gross margin (sales minus costs of goods sold) exceeding that of its competitors, that shows that it's doing something right, probably with its customers and/or with its costs. But unfortunately, it isn't *that* easy. Competitive analysis is elusive; it's hard to find a dependable source of "industry" gross margins, and comparing competitors can be difficult because no two companies are exactly alike; it's easy to mix apples and oranges.

I like to see what direction gross margin is moving in—up or down. A growing gross margin signals that the company is doing something right. A declining gross margin suggests stronger competition, higher input costs, or less-effective management. It also makes sense to consider the economic context: in a poor economy, companies that can protect their margins will come out ahead.

Incidentally, the *Value Line Investment Survey* research reports are an excellent way to track margin progress over time.

Does a Company Produce More Capital Than It Consumes?

Make no mistake about it, I like cash. And pure and simple, I like it when a company produces more cash than it consumes.

At the end of the day, cash generation is the simplest measure of whether a company is successful, especially over the long term. Sure, if a company buys an airplane or opens a factory or a bunch of stores in a given quarter, it will be cash-flow negative. But that should be a temporary thing; over the long haul, it should produce, not consume cash.

Companies that continually have to borrow or sell shares to raise enough cash to stay in business are on the wrong track. How do you determine this? You'll have to become familiar with the Statement of Cash Flows or equivalent in a company's financial reports. Again, see Habit 11: Look For Cash in All the Right Places.

Are Expenses in Line?

Just like your household, company expenses should be prudently managed and under control. Anything else, especially without explanation, is a yellow flag. The best way to test this is to check whether the "Selling, General, and Administrative" expenses (SG&A) are rising, and more to the point, are they rising faster than sales? If so, that's a yellow (not necessarily a red) flag, but if it continues, it suggests that something is out of control, and it will catch up with the company sooner or later.

In the recent recession, companies that were able to reduce their expenses to match revenue declines came out ahead. In more prosperous times, companies that grow expenses more slowly than sales become more profitable, As a result, they will be less vulnerable to the next downturn.

Does Working Capital Track the Business?

Working capital is a hard concept to grasp—even for small entrepreneurs who live with its ups and downs on a daily basis. Insufficient working capital is one of the biggest causes of death for small businesses, and working capital, especially changes in working capital, can signal success or trouble.

Using a simple analogy, working capital is the circulatory lifeblood of the business. Money comes in, money goes out, and working capital is what circulates in the veins in between. In its purest sense, it is cash, receivables, and inventory, less short-term debts. It's what you own less what you owe, aside from fixed assets such as plant, stores, and equipment.

If receivables are increasing, that sounds like a good thing—more people owe you more money. But if receivables are rising and sales aren't, that suggests that people aren't paying their bills, or worse, the business has to finance more to achieve the same level of sales. Similarly, a rise in inventory without a rise in sales means that it costs the business more money—more working capital—to do the same amount of business. Unless the firm is lucky, more inventory means more obsolescence and potentially more deep-discount sales or write-offs down the road – a double whammy.

So a sharp investor will check to see that major working capital items—receivables and inventory—aren't growing faster than sales. Indeed, a company that generates more sales without increasing working capital is becoming more efficient.

Does the Company Have Too Much Debt?

As with many other "fundamentals" items, you can tear your hair out looking at debt figures and trying to decide whether they're in line with asset levels, equity levels, and industry norms. A simpler test is to check and see whether long-term debt is increasing or decreasing. In particular, you should look at whether it is increasing faster than business growth. Gold stars go to companies with little to no debt and to companies able to grow without issuing mountains of long-term debt. No debt on the balance sheet at all? That's usually a good thing.

Does the Company Report *Consistently* Good Results?

We enter the danger zone here, because the management of many companies has learned to "manage" earnings to provide a steady improvement, always "beating the street" by a penny or two. So stability is a good thing for all investors, and companies that can manage toward stability get extra points. It's worth checking for, but with the proverbial grain of salt.

Still, a company that is able to manage its sales, earnings, cash flow, and debt levels more consistently than competitors, and perhaps more consistently than what would be suggested by the ups and downs of the economy, is desirable—or at least more desirable than the alternatives.

Get Into the Habit

- Remember that fundamentals are the scorecard of the past, while intangibles such as brand and marketplace, and management excellence foretell the scorecard of the future.
- Keep in mind that fundamentals measure absolute business performance, relative performance over time (trends), and efficiency.
- Use fundamentals as a measure of (1) how strong a company is in the marketplace and (2) how effectively management converts that strength into profits.
- Develop your own list of "strategic fundamentals" (starting with the one provided, if you want). Use that list as an "acid test" for companies you own or evaluate to buy.

Look for Cash in All the Right Places

Why do you invest? Well, to earn money, of course. *Make it, keep it, grow it*—that's what it's all about.

But suppose you "earned" money over time, but the only evidence of that was an accounting entry? A printed report? You own a company, but you never see a dime of the earnings flow into your own pocket. Instead, it's kept by the company as "retained earnings." Suppose further that those "earnings" were largely the result of an accounting transaction, say, the increased accounting valuation of assets owned, or the "goodwill" from an acquisition. Are these "gains" as good as cash in your pocket? Maybe so, but maybe not.

Over the long run, the only true measure of a company's success is the amount of cash it generates: cash in its pocket, which in time, should become cash in *your* pocket. These days it's not hard to find an example in which real cash was better than an arbitrary figure—consider what happened in the real estate boom. If you sold, you got real cash for your house. If you didn't, the gain in the price of your house was merely an exercise in valuation, which in this case proved to be wrong.

Mind you, I'm not saying that income, or "earnings," generated in a business is a bad thing. I'm just saying that cash is better. As a sharp investor, you should get in the habit of learning how the business performs on a cash basis, and you should expect to receive some of that cash once in a while.

Thus, as an investor, you should always pay attention to assets and income, but even closer attention to cash and debt.

• Does the company produce or consume cash?
• Does the company reward shareholders with cash?

Make a habit of reading the cash flow of a business. You'll want to do your "detective work" using the Statement of Cash Flows as the primary source.

Know the Difference Between Earnings and Cash

Cash is—well—cash. It is hard money earned and collected by a company in the course of business, and it is hard money spent and actually paid to acquire something, like eight hours of labor, a raw material input, or a building or machine needed to produce something.

So why aren't "earnings" and "cash" the same thing? Why are there separate income statements and statements of cash flow?

The difference is *timing*.

Suppose you're running an airline. You sell tickets and collect cash, usually from credit card companies, pretty much at exactly the same time as tickets are purchased. So, timing differences, if they exist at all, are very small. If you sell $100,000 in tickets in a given month, you'll probably receive $100,000 in cash. Revenues and cash are very closely matched.

But airlines fly airplanes, don't they? And airplanes are large and expensive purchases that might be made every twenty years or so. You spend $20 million for an airplane, and then don't do it again for twenty years. Does the expense match the cash flow?

Well, it could. But it wouldn't be a very good idea, for your airline would report excellent earnings for nineteen years, then a terrible loss in the year that the airplane is purchased or replaced.

To manage this, accountants have come up with the notion of *depreciation*. With depreciation, the $20 million purchase is spread out over the twenty years as annual expenses, perhaps at $1 million a year with so-called "straight line" depreciation, or perhaps with another formula allowed by the IRS. In this example, cash flows differ significantly from reported income, expenses, and earnings flows, because the latter have been adjusted for depreciation.

Now, depreciation is actually a good idea, and makes the business relatively more manageable from year to year. This sort of smoothing over also helps investors. But there are a lot of other transactions that use cash but may not have corresponding expenses, and investors need to be aware of those, too. If you're running a car dealership and spend cash to buy some inventory, are you recording any expense? No, for one asset is simply being turned into another. But you are consuming cash to buy inventory, and cash used to build inventories could be a very bad thing if done in excess.

The bottom line is that investors should watch *both* earnings and cash. The airline example is extreme because of the cost and useful life of an aircraft—but for all businesses, including airlines, over time cash flows should match earnings flows. Because of the other ways in which a business can use or produce cash, it also makes sense—and is, in fact, imperative—to watch cash flows. Accountants can gimmick earnings statements within the law, but over time they cannot gimmick cash. A company that does not produce enough cash will ultimately run out and will ultimately fail.

Read the Statement of Cash Flows

Many novice investors, if they read financial statements at all, stop at the Income Statement and Balance Sheet. These two statements tell a lot about the health of a business, and if you read them, that's good. But since many assets and expense items, such as depreciation and inventory buildups or drawdowns, either affect income arbitrarily or don't affect it at all, as a sharp investor you should complete the "triple play" and take a close look at the statement of cash flows.

Every company produces a statement of cash flows, and a rather typical one looks like Figure 11.1, the Statement of Cash Flows for the Procter & Gamble Company for the three years 2009–2011. (Quarterly cash flow statements are also available.)

FIGURE 11.1: STATEMENT OF CASH FLOWS— THE PROCTER & GAMBLE COMPANY

Period Ending	June 30, 2011	June 30, 2010	June 30, 2009
Net Income	$11,797,000	$12,736,000	$13,436,000
Cash Flows Provided By or Used in Operating Activities			
Depreciation	$2,838,000	$3,108,000	$3,082,000
Adjustments to Net Income	$339,000	($2,181,000)	($1,265,000)
Changes in Accounts Receivable	($426,000)	($14,000)	$415,000
Changes in Liabilities	$358,000	$2,446,000	($742,000)
Changes in Inventories	($501,000)	$86,000	$721,000
Changes in Other Operating Activities	($1,174,000)	($109,000)	($728,000)

FIGURE 11.1: STATEMENT OF CASH FLOWS—
THE PROCTER & GAMBLE COMPANY

Total Case Flow From Operating Activities	$13,231,000	$16,072,000	$14,919,000
Cash Flows Provided By or Used in Investing Activities			
Capital Expenditures	($3,306,000)	($3,067,000)	($3,238,000)
Investments	$73,000	($173,000)	$166,000
Other Cash Flows From Investing Activities	($249,000)	$2,643,000	$719,000
Total Cash Flows From Investing Activities	($3,482,000)	($597,000)	($2,353,000)
Cash Flows Provided By or Used in Financing Activities			
Dividends Paid	($5,767,000)	($5,458,000)	($5,044,000)
Sale or Purchase of Stock	($5,737,000)	($5,283,000)	($5,689,000)
Net Borrowings	$1,481,000	($6,514,000)	($81,000)
Other Cash Flows From Financing Activities	–	–	–
Total Cash Flows From Financing Activities	($10,023,000)	($17,255,000)	($10,814,000)
Effect of Exchange Rate Changes	$163,000	($122,000)	($284,000)
Change in Cash or Cash Equivalents	($111,000)	($1,902,000)	($1,468,000)

Now, is P&G producing more cash than it consumes? Are shareholders enjoying any benefits from P&G's cash generation? Does cash appear to be well managed?

The answer to all three questions is "yes." To get there, let's walk through the statement.

First, for the three annual periods, we see P&G's reported Net Income—the net earnings achieved through traditional accounting methods. The Statement of Cash Flows shows adjustments to this figure to account for cash and non-cash income and expense items, such as depreciation, asset revaluation, and transfer between types of assets. From this "top line" number, there are three categories of adjustments:

Cash Flow from ("Provided By or Used By") Operating Activities

Cash flow from operating activities typically reflects the "cash register" from day-to-day operations. How much was received from customers, and how much was paid out directly to produce products, are accounted for here. Unless the company is really doing badly, the figure is usually positive and represents cash booked from sales less cost of goods sold, with adjustments for noncash items such as depreciation and for increases or decreases in working capital items like inventory and receivables. In this example, P&G booked $2.8 billion in depreciation as an expense in 2011, but this is an accounting transaction; no cash left the company, so true cash flow, so far, is the $11.797 billion in net income plus the $2.838 billion in depreciation expense for which no cash went out.

Working capital adjustments include a *negative* $501 million for inventory. That means cash was *used* to purchase inventory. If that number had been positive, that would mean inventory would have *dropped* by $501 million, generating cash through its sale equivalent to that amount—a positive cash flow. The bottom line: after making some adjustments for working capital, there was a net cash gain from operations of $13.321 billion.

That's great, but are we done? We still don't have the bottom line for cash, only what happened in operations. The company's daily business operations, though, are indeed generating a lot of cash. Next, we go on to:

Cash Used for Investing Activities

This category is a bit of a misnomer and represents net cash used to "invest" in the business—usually for capital expenditures, but also for short-term noncash investments like securities and a few other smaller items beyond our scope. This figure is typically negative unless the company sells some part of its infrastructure. Over the long haul, cash generated from operations should well exceed cash used to invest in the business, unless a company is in heavy expansion mode.

Note that funds used to acquire capital equipment are shown here, as the equipment is actually purchased, just as in the airplane example cited at the beginning.

Cash Flow from Financing Activities

Companies, particularly those in expansion mode, may not show a surplus of operating cash flow over investing cash flow. That's where financing cash flow comes in.

Cash from financing activities is the cash generated from issuing debt or selling securities—or used for paying off debt or repurchasing shares, if things are going well, and dividends are included here as well. Again, a successful company will produce more cash—capital—from the business than it consumes, just as a successful household does the same, or else it goes into debt. Smart investors track this surplus over time.

In this example, P&G generated a little over $13 billion in cash from operations, and used a little over $3 billion mostly to invest in its business assets. That left about $10 billion to add to the cash hoard on the balance sheet. Did P&G do that? No—they paid about $5 billion in dividends and then paid out another $5 billion to repurchase shares on the open market, thus making remaining shares more valuable for current owners. The bottom line was an almost unchanged cash balance—it dropped only $111 million to a figure of about $2.8 billion, not shown here but on the balance sheet.

Does P&G Pass the Smell Test?

The statement of cash flows just examined suggests a healthy business situation. Procter & Gamble's operating cash flows were strong and achieved without big changes in working capital items, like inventory or receivables growth. Operating cash funded capital expenditures ("CapEx") with plenty left over, and what was left over was paid out almost entirely to shareholders. From a cash flow standpoint, especially because these figures are relatively consistent over the years, P&G is a company you would want to own.

IS CASH *ALL* YOU WANT TO LOOK AT?

Sharp investors learn to look for companies that, over time, produce capital, in contrast to companies that consume it. As judged by the statement of cash flows, a company that produces more cash from operations than it consumes in investing activities (capital equipment purchases mainly) and in financing activities (repaying debt, dividends, etc.) is producing capital. When a company must always go to the capital markets to make up for a deficit in operating or investing cash flow, that's a sign of trouble, which is incidentally borne out by the other absolute measure—debt. If debt is high and increasing, especially if it is increasing faster than the business is growing, look out. Or at least, look for a story: for instance, company XYZ is going through a known, understood, and rational expansion that needs to be funded. Going to the capital markets to fund operating cash deficits is an especially bad thing to do.

Of Particular Note: Sale or Purchase of Stock

Especially over the past few years, companies have become huge cash generation machines. The relatively slow economic growth rate and the maturation of major technologies such as information technology means that companies need to buy less and invest less to conduct ordinary business. The recent recession put an exclamation point on the need to "rightsize" and become efficient, so companies did this in a big way. The result was a huge increase in cash generation and cash reserves. It got to the point where investors became fed up with companies hoarding the cash (which also occurred because of complex U.S. tax laws regarding the repatriation of moneys earned overseas). Companies started to return to shareholders by buying back shares in the open market. Cash was paid to buy shares and retire them, making remaining shares more valuable. Companies *spent* billions doing this.

I've gotten in the habit of reviewing share repurchases, and it has become a major condition for choosing a stock (as in my *100 Best Stocks To Buy* lists, for example). If a company is buying back shares, it is (1) generating lots of free cash ("free" cash is cash beyond CapEx requirements), and (2) returning it to shareholders. Perhaps I'd like dividends better, because they represent real cash in hand, but steady repurchases and gains in the value of remaining shares aren't a bad thing.

The Statement of Cash Flows provides a rather handy window into the dollar amounts of share repurchases (or issuance, for companies going the other way either in the open market or through employee stock options). I've also gotten into the habit of looking at the *number* of shares outstanding over time. The *Value Line Investment Survey* is an excellent source for this figure.

It's truly amazing how many big American corporations have reduced their share counts 20 percent, 30 percent, or even more over the past ten years.

Get Into the Habit

- Make the Statement of Cash Flows part of your normal review process.
- Determine whether the company is producing or consuming cash (capital).
- Determine if cash flows are well managed and in control.
- Check to see that the company is returning cash to investors on a regular basis.

HABIT 12

Don't Forget the Intangibles

Warren Buffett has said many a wise thing about investing but none wiser than this:

> *"If you gave me $100 billion and said, 'Take away the soft drink leadership of Coca-Cola in the world,' I'd give it back to you and tell you that it can't be done."*

What did he mean by this statement? Simply this: Good businesses have intangible strengths and qualities that simply cannot be purchased at any price. They are difficult, if not impossible, to quantify, reproduce, or copy by competitors in the marketplace.

Moreover, these intangible qualities tend to be leading indicators of a company's success. You can easily look at intangibles such as brand, market position, customer loyalty, innovation strength, channel strength, and management to determine, at least to a degree, how well the company will do financially down the road. At the risk of oversimplifying, financials are the past, while intangibles are the future.

As you appraise any company as a possible investment, you should get into the habit of examining both the financials and the intangibles that make the company tick.

Strategic Intangibles

When you look at any company, perhaps the bottom-line question follows the Buffett wisdom: If you yourself had a hundred billion in cool cash to spend—and the genius intellect to spend it right—*could* you recreate that company?

If the answer is "yes," it may still be a great company, but it may not be great enough to fend off competition and keep its customers forever. If the answer is "no," the company truly has something unique to offer in the marketplace, difficult to duplicate at any cost. That sustainable competitive edge— whether it's a brand, a trade secret, or a lock on distribution or supply channels, may be worth more than all the factories, high-rise office buildings. and cash in the bank a company could ever have.

Intangibles are the "soft" factors that make companies unique. They add up to more than the sum of their parts; they're the factors that define excellence and future financial results. *Strategic* intangibles are among the many that are so important; they shouldn't be overlooked. Here are questions you should ask about seven key intangibles. (These seven are the most important for most businesses and industries, although some industries may have some unique ones, such as intellectual property in the technology sector.)

Does the Company Have a Moat?

As you're looking at the intangibles, you should ask yourself whether the company has a "moat?" and if so, is it a "wide" or a "narrow" one. What do I mean by a "moat?"

A business "moat" performs much the same role as its medieval equivalent—it protects the business from competition. Whatever factors—which are mostly intangibles—that create the moat, ultimately those are the ones that prevent you, armed though you may be with Mr. Buffett's $100 billion to invest, from taking their business. Moats are usually a combination of brand, product technology, design, marketing and distribution channels, and customer loyalty all working together to protect a company. A moat doesn't just protect the existence of a company, it helps it command higher prices and earn higher profits.

Whether a company has a "narrow" moat, a "wide" moat, or none at all is a subjective assessment you must make. However, you can get some help at Morningstar (*www.morningstar.com*), whose stock ratings include an assessment of the moat.

Coca-Cola has a moat because of the sheer impossibility of surpassing its brand and brand recognition worldwide. Intel has a moat because of its lead in microprocessor design and has unbeatable brand recognition. CarMax has a moat because it is further along in putting retail-style dealerships on the ground and applying management information technologies to its business than anyone else is; it would take years for a competitor to catch up. Tiffany has a moat because of its immediately recognized brand and elegantly simple, stylish brand image and the enduring and timeless panache around that.

The moat, usually defined by its intangibles taken as a whole, represents a company's competitive advantage. A company without a moat is basically producing a commodity and typically has little to compete on besides price.

Does the Company Have an Excellent Brand?

It's hard to say enough about brand, especially in today's fast-moving, highly packaged, highly national and international marketplace. A strong brand means consistency and a promise to consumers, and consumers sold on a brand will prefer it over any other, almost regardless of price. People still buy Tide; Starbucks is still synonymous with high quality and ambience. Good brands command higher prices and foster loyalty and identity—even customer "love."

Ask yourself if a company has a sought-after brand, a brand customers would pay extra to buy or align with, a brand that would be difficult to duplicate at any cost. Would customers rather fight than switch? Think about Starbucks, Coca-Cola, Heinz, Tiffany, Nike, or the brands within a house, like Frito-Lay (Pepsi), Tide (P&G), or Teflon (DuPont). Don't forget about brands in the business-to-business marketplace either—Caterpillar, 3M, Lubrizol, Safety-Kleen, Fastenal, SENCO and others.

Is the Company a Market Leader?

Market leadership usually, but not always, goes hand in hand with brand. The trick is to decide whether a company really leads in its industry. Often, but not always, that's a factor of size. The market leader usually has the highest market share, and the important point is that it calls the shots with regard to price, technology, marketing message, and so forth—other companies must play catch-up and often discount their prices to keep up. Apple is a market leader in personal electronics and digital music, Intel is the market leader in microprocessors, and Whirlpool is the market leader in home appliances.

Excellent companies tend to be market leaders, and market leaders tend to be excellent companies. But this relationship doesn't always hold true—sometimes the nimble but smaller competitor is the excellent company and will likely assume market leadership eventually. Examples such as CarMax, Nucor, Perrigo, Valero, and Southwest Airlines are easy to spot.

Successful investors also think about market *positioning.*
Is the company a price leader? A quality leader? A customer
service leader? Does it represent the low end (Walmart), the
high end (Nordstrom), or the middle (Target)? Is it clear
what part of the market it targets? Does it do it well? Is it the
leader in that space? The marketplace is littered with unsuc-
cessful companies that either couldn't figure out what they
stood for, or couldn't achieve it once decided. More on this in
Habit 13: Put on Your Marketing Hat.

Does the Company Have Loyal Customers?

You won't know for sure, but a quick examination of the
marketplace—and your own experiences—might give a clue
about whether customers would rather fight than switch. Esti-
mates from the mobile phone industry and others indicate
that it costs about seven times as much to acquire a new customer as to retain an existing one, so a company that has loyalty is doing something right. Loyalty can be created by, or
goes hand in hand with, brand, as in the case of Starbucks. It
can be created by solid customer service (Sears, John Deere,
Caterpillar) or by product excellence, innovation, and design
(Apple and Tiffany).

Also note whether companies do things to damage their
reputations, and observe what (if anything) they do about it.
Many become public spectacles, such as BP during the Gulf
oil-spill disaster; these are eventually handled well and at
some point cease to cost the company. Damage can also be
very small and localized—even in things as simple as customer
service (Starbucks' reputation for long lines, for instance).
It's good to observe what companies do about such inhibitors
and how fast and well they do it.

Does the Company Innovate?

Most of us associate innovations with technology and technology companies, which are in the business of inventing and selling things that make business and personal life easier, better, or faster. But innovation goes far beyond the products that a company sells. And it isn't just about ideas—many companies "invent"—that is, develop new things and may even patent them. But far fewer "innovate"—that is, create new things that economically solve a customer problem and will, as a result, succeed in the marketplace.

Smart investors sniff out innovation and decide whether a company's innovations and innovation habits are a competitive advantage.

Innovation isn't just about products and widgets sold at your local big box electronics outlet. It can also be, and it may be, a real source of competitive advantage about whether a company makes the best *use* of technology to make operations and customer interfaces as efficient and effective as possible. Companies that don't seem so innovative on the surface may turn out to be on closer examination. UPS, for example, is current developing a system with which customers can schedule their own deliveries online within a delivery window. This will greatly increase UPS's preference for valuable e-commerce shipments to busy people.

Be careful here, however. Just because a company has an innovation, it doesn't mean that it will lead to market—and ultimately financial—success. UPS may have a good idea and may have emphasized it in their company PR and advertising. But can the company actually execute on the innovation; that is, does it work? How easy, and how *quickly*, can the competition copy it? Will FedEx roll out the same service feature two months later? Innovations must be leading, useful, effective, and sustainable to really count—otherwise all that the company is really doing is keeping up.

Some innovations are particularly subtle but effective. Southwest Airlines excels today not only because of brand and management excellence, but also because of innovation excellence. Why? Simply because, after all of these years, they still have the best, simplest, and easiest-to-use flight booking and check-in in the industry. The innovation seems to be just as much about design and customer experience as it is about technology, but it works. Sometimes these sorts of innovations mean a lot more than bringing new, fancy products with bells and whistles to the market.

Does the Company Have Channel Excellence?

"Channels" in business parlance means a chain of players to sell and distribute a company's products. It might be stores; it might be other industrial companies; it might be direct to the consumer. If a company is considered a top supplier in a particular channel or a company has especially good relations with its channel, that's a plus.

Excellent companies develop solid channel relationships and become the preferred supplier in those channels. Companies such as Nike, Pepsi, Procter & Gamble, and Whirlpool all have excellent relationships with the channels through which they sell their product.

Does the Company Have Supply Chain Excellence?

Like distribution channels, excellent companies develop excellent low-cost supply channels. They are seldom caught off guard by supply shortages and tend to get favorable and stable prices for whatever they buy. This is often not an easy assessment unless you know something about a particular industry. Nike and Target are good examples of companies that have done a good job of managing their supply chains.

Does the Company Have Excellent Management?

Well, it's not hard to grasp what happens if a company *doesn't* have good management; performance fails and few inside or outside the company respect the company. It's not easy for an investor to determine if a management team does a good job or acts in shareholder interests. Clues can include candor and honesty and the ability of company management to speak in accessible, easily understood terms about the company and company performance. (It's worth listening to conference calls as a resource.) A management team that admits errors and eschews other forms of arrogance and entitlement (e.g., luxury perks, office suites, aircraft) is probably tilting its interests toward shareholders. So too is the management team that can cough up some return to shareholders once in a while in the form of a dividend.

This may be the most subjective and elusive assessment of all, as few investors work with these folks on a daily basis. Still, over time, you can garner a strong hunch about whether a management team is effective and on your side. For more see Habit 15: Sense the Management Style.

Absorbing It All

While most sources of investing information present at least some of the key financial information you'd look for, it can be harder to gather information on intangibles. Most financial reports contain only bits and pieces of material listed above. Certainly none do it in a manner that follows this outline.

So what to do? You'll have to be creative. You'll have to track the financial media, look at company websites and reports, listen to what people have to say about their experiences with the company, and become familiar with the industry. Getting a picture of the intangibles is more about absorption, interpretation, and experience than it is about reading lists of facts.

You'll want to read what the company says about itself, see how it presents itself and behaves in the marketplace, and hear what others have to say about it.

The outline just presented will help—just ask yourself whether a company has an excellent brand, a solid market position, good innovation, solid management, and so forth. You may answer some definitively, while others will be an "I don't know." That's okay, and over time you'll pick up signals that strengthen your assessment. If *most* of your answers are "I don't know," however, you might want to stay away from the investment, at least for now.

WHY CAN'T I GET THIS STRAIGHT FROM THE COMPANY?

Wouldn't it be nice if the SEC required companies to report these intangibles in their financial statements and annual reports, using some sort of common format like this? Well, chances are, companies would fight such a rule, because it would get to the core of what many might consider proprietary information or secrets.

If companies had to report on intangibles . . . well, it might be a pretty intangible report, as much of it goes beyond simple facts to an interpretation or explanation of a lot of experience and events. It is a *story*. And as we all know, stories can be altered and embellished to say what we want to say and what we want people to hear.

Get Into the Habit

- Recognize and realize that intangibles are about the future, while financials are about the past.
- Look for "moats"—sustainable competitive advantages.
- Examine, one by one, the following (some may be more elusive than others):

  - Brand
  - Market leadership and position
  - Customer loyalty
  - Innovation excellence
  - Channel excellence
  - Supply chain excellence
  - Management excellence

- Absorb intangible information by regularly reading about the company in the news, visits to the company and/or its websites, and listening to what others—personal or professional—have to say about the company.

HABIT 13

Put on Your Marketing Hat

When you read any book about investing, you're likely to read a lot about financials: sales, earnings, cash flow, balance sheet, price-to-earnings ratios, and so forth. No doubt, these fundamentals are important, but I find that most investing books stop short of really helping you understand a *business*.

If you read Habit 12: Don't Forget the Intangibles, you already have a pretty good idea that there is a lot more to a business than the financials, particularly if you're trying to predict the future, which is in fact what most of us investors are doing. Financials are a mirror into the past, while a company's intangibles are a spyglass into the future.

Among the most important intangibles in predicting the future is marketing. How does the company position itself compared to its competition? How does it position and price its products? How—and how well—does it acquire and retain customers? Does it have a solid brand? Does it control its marketplace well enough to raise prices and thus profits? What are its greatest strengths and weaknesses in its markets? What are the opportunities and threats?

These are some of the questions that sharp investors habitually ask about their investments and prospective investments. These are questions about the company's markets and marketing. They're about a company's *strategic* marketing, which involves decisions about how to develop, position, and price products and services, and its *tactical* marketing—how it actually presents itself to the marketplace.

As a habit, I suggest that you put on your marketing hat when evaluating an investment. Pretend, at least for a few minutes, that you're the Chief Marketing Officer for that business. This "habit" cannot possibly be a complete marketing course, but here's a quick overview of some of the concepts and tools good marketers use.

Is the Company Positioned for Success?

Positioning refers to how a company wants to play and develop its products and services for the marketplace. It is how a company wants to *compete*. Is the company competing on price alone or some other basis? Does the company have a solid portfolio of products or is it a one-hit wonder? Is service an important part of the offering? Location? Customer experience?

You might think of it as you would think of three big retailers: Walmart, Target, and Nordstrom. Walmart is the low-price leader with a strategy of establishing stores everywhere, high volumes, and low margins. At the other end is Nordstrom (or Neiman Marcus or another high-end retailer you might be familiar with locally) with relatively high prices, exclusive brands, and high-touch service. Target falls somewhere in between—more elegant merchandise, more pleasant shopping conditions, some but not high-touch service, and moderate prices. As an example, when you size up a business, decide whether it's the Walmart, Nordstrom, or Target of the industry. Of course, there are other continuums you can use.

Once you decide how a company is positioned, ask yourself how strong the competition is in that position or segment, and whether the company you're evaluating is succeeding, failing, or if it falls somewhere in between.

Look for Niche Players

A *niche*, in marketing, is a small but meaningful segment of a market that can be dominated by a single company. That dominance allows the company to dictate the market, that is, to set the price and what's offered for the price. In many cases, the company is so important and visible to that niche that it doesn't really have to advertise or market its services.

Coffee purveyor Starbucks is a good example. The coffee market is deep and wide, but Starbucks in the beginning saw a niche for high-quality coffee served in a pleasant, upscale, European-style environment. They dominated that niche and did a lot of other things well, too, becoming a third place beyond the home and traditional workplace for on-the-go workers, moms, and college students. For millions, they effectively replaced the neighborhood tavern. They have come to dominate the high-end, locally-served coffee niche, commanding higher prices than the competition with virtually no advertising.

Many other successful companies dominate their niches too, whether it is with products, service, or simply location. When evaluating a company, ask yourself whether it dominates any niches, or if it must compete head to head with other strong challengers for a much broader market. Good players in good niches tend to make good investments—especially when the niche becomes an entire market—as the Starbucks and Apples of the world have found.

Does the Company Have a Solid Product Portfolio?

A company that sells good products to good niches in growing markets will do well. A company that sells bad or "me too" products to flat or declining markets, with no "niche" presence or pricing power, will find itself in an eternal struggle.

Marketers use all sorts of tools to analyze and diagram their businesses. It seems that almost anything in business— or in life, for that matter—can be put in four quadrants to help figure it out and make the right decisions. (Interestingly, psychologists like to do this too.)

One of the more popular grids in use in business today was created and used by the Boston Consulting Group way back in 1970. It is called a "growth-share matrix" or more informally, a "BCG Box or simply a "Boston Box."

Figure 13.1 illustrates a basic Boston Box. Here's how it works. You take a product—or an assortment of products— and position it according to the matrix. If it has a high market share in a high-growth market, it is a "Star." You can think of anything that Apple makes today as a "Star," with the possible exception of MacBooks, which still might be considered a "Question Mark" with high-growth and relatively low (but growing!) market share. How do you know the growth and share numbers? It's very difficult, but you can get an idea from what you observe in the marketplace and/or what you read in the financial press.

FIGURE 13.1: THE BOSTON BOX MATRIX

Stars		*Question Marks*
Cash Cows		*Dogs*

High Growth / Low Growth

High Market Share   Low Market Share

Finally, we have "Dogs" with low growth and low market share—products most companies would likely want to either get rid of or do better with. Interesting is the "Cash Cow"—low-growth products that produce high margins—likely because the company dominates a niche. Drug companies have a lot of cash cows, which are "milked" to produce cash to invest in R&D for new drugs. Big SUVs were cash cows for U.S. auto companies until they got sick on high gas prices.

The intention of this exercise is to look at a company's products and decide if most are stars, cash cows (good), question marks (?) or dogs (bad). Again, a lot of this will be based on your intuition and is hard to quantify, but it helps you to decide whether a company is on the right track.

Consider a simple example I did for Hewlett-Packard, shown in Figure 13.2. The company has clear examples of products in all four quadrants (not every company will). Its "Blade Servers," the simple servers designed to scale up capacity in a data center, website installation, etc., are one of its "star" products, offering high margins in a high-growth market. (Again, it helps to read a lot or have a "smart friend" in the business to help.) Its network storage products are in a rapidly growing market, but the company has relatively low share, so those products are question marks. The ink cartridges have long been a cash cow—very profitable products but in today's world, a very slow growing market. Finally, PCs could be the dogs. HP does have the number one worldwide market share position, but with less than 20 percent share, it doesn't really reap the benefits of high share.

FIGURE 13.2: BOSTON BOX MATRIX—HEWLETT-PACKARD

	High Market Share	**Low Market Share**
High Growth	*Stars* • Blade servers	*Question Marks* • Network storage
Low Growth	• Ink Cartridges *Cash Cows*	• PCs *Dogs*

HP as a whole is kind of a question mark itself. The cash cow ink cartridge market may actually be declining as tablets replace print volume and competitors refill cartridges cheaply. Part of the exercise is to determine *direction*—for instance, are cash cows or stars losing their cash cow or star status?

In fact, sometimes it helps to simply place *the whole company* within this framework. HP is probably, as a whole, somewhere between a dog and a question mark, while Apple is clearly a star. Starbucks might be somewhere between a star and a cash cow, and most utilities and energy companies are obvious cash cows. Chipotle Mexican Grill is somewhere between a question mark and a star; unless you define its market narrowly as the "hand-made, you-pick-it" burrito market, it is still a minor share player in a huge fast-food market.

Naturally, you want to buy stars or question marks if you have a high-risk tolerance and cash cows if you have a lower risk tolerance. Companies that fund star products with cash cow cash, like drug makers and, in the old days, HP, are usually a good bet—if they're using their cash wisely.

Product Evolution? Or Just a Flash in the Pan?

Some companies are one-trick ponies. They sell one product and sell it well. Sometimes that product has a quick rise and fall in the marketplace, like netbook computers or video rentals, and sometimes it lasts forever. Other companies have a well-thought-out and well-executed product evolution. The evolutionary path makes sense, retains or even increases customer loyalty, and in the best cases, becomes widely anticipated and generates excitement. (Again, think of those masters of the marketing universe, Apple.)

Restaurants, especially new restaurant concepts, are notorious for being flash-in-the-pan, one-trick ponies that ultimately crash and burn (anyone remember Victoria Station?). Some appear that way but find ways to continue and build (many thought Starbucks was simply a trendy thing that would disappear). I'm still not sure that Chipotle is here to stay, but it's really in vogue at the time of this writing. Software companies also flirt with this danger, unless they command their niche and keep developing good follow-on products (e.g., Microsoft, Adobe).

Try, as a marketer/investor, to visualize where a company's products might be five years from now, in an era of ever-more-rapid change in technology and consumer tastes.

Is the Company Gaining or Losing Share?

As touched on above, whether a company has high or low market share is important. Just as important—maybe more so—is whether the company is *gaining* or *losing* share. Again, this can be inferred from reading the press or just seeing what's going on "on the street." Are there fewer HP products on the shelves at retailers these days? Share may be in trouble.

*Mind*share is also important. As marketers like to say, it's all about the "share of customer" or "share of wallet" belonging to that customer. Is the company a hero to its customers, as is Apple or John Deere or Costco? Or is it likely to be thrown to the winds as soon as another competitor comes along or if one lowers the price a buck or two? How strong is the affinity between the company and its customers? And is it getting better (Apple) or getting worse (Sears, Toyota, Netflix)?

Bottom line: Is the company winning in the marketplace? Winning with customers?

Does the Company Present Itself Effectively?

This one seems pretty obvious, but if you like how the company presents itself to the public, mainly through advertising, its web presence, and in some cases, its public relations and press releases, chances are others will like it too. Companies with weak, boring, or muddied messages just don't work in today's world of information overload and quick uptake.

Clear, creative, insightful, informative messages that convey value work; bland, confusing, self-serving messages that show no value (like many from the oil industry, for instance) generally don't. Stick with the companies that have a solid and well-communicated message.

Think SWOT

Finally, we get to an exercise played not only by marketers but by business leaders in executive suites everywhere—the SWOT (Strengths, Weaknesses, Opportunities, Threats) analysis. As Figure 13.3 shows, it's really pretty simple. Just analyze each company for what you see as its Strengths (helpful characteristics internal to the company, like lots of cash or strong brands or great products), and its Weaknesses (self-inflicted harmful characteristics like debt, bad products, high warranty costs, high input costs, poor sales channels, etc.).

FIGURE 13.3: SWOT ANALYSIS FRAMEWORK.

	Helpful	*Harmful*
Internal	**S***trengths*	**W***eaknesses*
External	**O***pportunities*	**T***hreats*

Once you have these "internal" characteristics down, move on to the "Opportunities" and "Threats" in the marketplace. I've furnished an example, again for HP, in Figure 13.4:

FIGURE 13.4: SWOT ANALYSIS FOR HEWLETT-PACKARD

	Helpful	Harmful
Internal	**S**trengths • Strong brand recognition • Size and scale • International presence	**W**eaknesses • Size, difficult to manage • Weak on innovation • 6 CEOs in 10 years
External	• Asian markets • Integrated tablets & PCs • Replacement cycle for aging IT infrastructure **O**pportunities	• Apples and tablets • Declining printing volumes • Oracle hardware/software integration **T**hreats

Note that I have limited each quadrant to three items, the ones I consider most important. Doubtless there are others, and you can probably think of others when you consider your companies. You may want to list them all or may want to do as I did and cut them down to the most important among the many.

As you do this, you'll want to think about whether any of the Weaknesses or Threats are absolute showstoppers, like an exceptionally weak financial position or obsolete technology. Again, like much else in marketing, it's a matter of judgment but can be helped along by personal observation and expert opinions.

Get Into the Habit

- Think about companies you own—or want to buy—as a marketer would.
- Decide where the company positions itself (Walmart-Target-Nordstrom as an example), and decide whether the company is succeeding with this positioning.
- Look for solid niche players and signs of niche leadership.
- Look at a company's product portfolio—and the company itself—to seek out Stars and Cash Cows.
- Determine if the company is gaining share—and share (mindshare) of customer.
- Decide whether the company presents itself clearly and effectively in the marketplace. Does it convey value to its customers?
- Identify three Strengths, Weaknesses, Opportunities, and Threats for each company. Decide if any of the Weaknesses or Threats are showstoppers.

HABIT 14

Put on Your Street Shoes

If you've been reading along in sequence, you're probably a bit overwhelmed by Habit 12: Don't Forget the Intangibles and Habit 13: Put on Your Marketing Hat. That's totally understandable. For those of you not trained or experienced in the art and science of the business world, it's been a challenging short crash course in a difficult, nuanced topic. Intangibles are—well—intangible.

You're excused if you're confused.

So I'd like to get back to a shorter and more basic habit touched on earlier. Instead of being a marketer, which is often a six-figure-plus job in a major corporation, let's be a *marketee*. Let's put ourselves in the position of a customer shopping for, and perhaps buying, a company's products. Whereas being a good marketer requires a lot of specialized education and skills, being a marketee requires nothing but your six senses and a pair of shoes. Anybody can do it.

Your job is to think like a customer: a customer of a company you might be evaluating. How is the company perceived by you, the customer? What is the *experience* offered by the company? Will you love that company? Will you love the experience? Or will you hate their guts?

I know this is a more difficult assessment with, say, a company such as Stryker that makes orthopedic implants. You probably have no experience, and little to no way of getting any experience (thank goodness!). You may have to live it through others, read about it online, talk to a health-care professional or two—be creative.

Likewise, you may not get that "customer" feel the next time you buy a tank of gas—gas is gas, after all. Or is it? How clean were the restrooms? If you live near a refinery, does it look like a lot of tank cars are being switched in and out, or are the yards empty? (You laugh, or maybe sigh. But Warren Buffett famously did this back in his early days—counting tank cars being switched in and out of a local chemical plant he was studying.)

So get your eyeballs out, put on a pair of shoes, and hit the street. Hit the mall, hit the city, hit the farm fields or feed stores if you're looking at John Deere or Monsanto. Look at their facilities and the online presence. Talk to salespeople, customer service agents, and other company representatives or channel partners (as in a Best Buy sales rep if you're looking for opinions about computer companies, or the doctor familiar with orthopedic implants). Talk to smart friends and industry experts.

Most of all: stop, look, and listen.

Look at the Facilities

Okay, this isn't going to work for everything. They aren't going to let you into the drug research lab, and if you live in Manhattan, you're a long way from a John Deere dealership. Nevertheless, there are always ways to get clues from direct observation. Being there is best, but pictures can tell a lot too.

Get a general impression; also, here's a short list of specifics to look for:

- *Are they busy?* Go to a Starbucks. Is it crowded? Do people seem happy? Is it busy just first thing in the morning, or also at off times during the day? Do retail stores seem busy? Parking lots full? Auto dealerships full of people? Are there a lot of trucks backed up at the shipping dock of a factory or warehouse? Continuous sampling is important here—you might just catch an off time or an off location. Check out the facilities near you. Check out other facilities when you travel. Ask your friends what they experienced at the Starbucks they visited.

- *Are they organized?* Neat, clean, well-organized, well-maintained, and well-merchandised facilities reflect good management, sufficient funds to pay the costs of being clean and organized, and a sensitivity towards the customer experience. A store with scattered merchandise, poor price marking, potholed parking lots, and dirty windows and restrooms shouts indifference about customers. Similarly, unkempt factory or warehouse buildings signify inattentiveness, or worse, not enough cash to spiff things up. I know—many a chemical or oil company has made bundles of money with ugly, overgrown, unkempt facilities, but if I had to choose the outfit with a better chance, I'd pick the tidy one!

- *Are they customer focused?* Does the help seem friendly, helpful, and courteous? Are the facilities well lit and well laid out? Is it easy to find things? Do people have to wait in long lines? (I could have foretold the Borders Group bankruptcy fifteen years before it happened based solely on the amount of time they were

willing to have a customer wait in line at check out.)
Are telephone support centers friendly and personal,
or are they automated, impersonal, and take forever to
get to a human? Sure, I've had boorish service in the
past, even from companies such as Apple, but again, if
you have a choice, stick to those that provide a pleasant, friendly, helpful experience. And again, don't be
afraid to ask your family, friends, and acquaintances
about their experiences.

* *Help, not hype.* When you go into a local bank branch,
do they help you? Or do they spend most of their time
(and your time) trying to sell you some new product
or service off of a poorly conceived, clumsy script?
Does every contact become a marketing confrontation?
Companies that truly want customers to get what they
want or need don't blitz you with unwanted messaging
(by phone or text or e-mail, let alone in person) along
the way. Companies that have really good products or
service don't need to do this.

Look at the Online Presence

Does the experience "click?" Looking at a company's website
can tell a lot about how the company perceives itself, and
what kind of experience it intends for its customers.

No two websites are alike (wouldn't it be boring if they
were?) Some are arty—too arty, too full of fancy features to
really be helpful. But most companies do a good job today of
describing who they are, what products they sell, where they
sell them, how they work, how they help you, and where to get
more information about them.

There are no specific guidelines here, but I look for
websites that tell what you need to know about a company's

products, its innovations, and how they will benefit *you*. Some websites get carried away with telling us how good the company is to its community; others are so loaded with buzzwords and industry jargon that we can't really figure out what the heck they *are* talking about. Some have very poor navigation. Some are simply glitzy brochures that don't really say much of anything. If the message isn't clear or isn't about value, if it does little or nothing to explain the company, its products, or how they will benefit you, it's a mark against the company.

Watch the Advertisements

I know—ads are usually boring, salesy, and not something you want to spend a lot of time looking at on a Sunday morning, unless you're in the market for something. But ads can tell a lot about a business and how it wants to be perceived by customers And they can tell a lot about a company's position in the marketplace.

For instance, does a company have a top-rate image in the industry or dominate its niche in such a way that it can control price? If so, price will scarcely be mentioned, if at all. Ever see anything about price in an Apple ad? In contrast, some companies compete on nothing *but* price and are constantly blitzing you with the latest sale and bragging of the lowest price out there. These companies don't control price, and thus have thin margins, made thinner by all that advertising they have to pay for.

Some ads are about companies or a company image, not a specific product. I brought up some of those oil company ads spreading the environmental awareness message—nice, but are they really about value? Or just a PR exercise designed to make you hate them less? You be the judge, but digging itself out of a hate position isn't such a good place to be for a business and should make you think twice about owning a piece of it.

Sometimes, little to no advertising is really the best path. This shows that the company has loyal and satisfied customers, and that the buzz is positive. I was actually a bit disappointed to see Starbucks crank up its ad spending a few years ago during its restructuring. It seemed like its nearly ad-less strategy was working pretty well. Let the product sell itself, and if it does, you'll sell more product for higher prices and save lots of money on advertising. That appeared to be the thinking, anyway.

Some ads project not only a product, but also an indelible image, and can work wonders for a company. No ad has ever impressed or moved me more than the Chrysler 2011 Super Bowl "Imported From Detroit" commercial starring Eminem. Apparently it impressed a lot of others, too, for it tripled the sales of the car model being presented.

Ask yourself—are the ads a positive? Or are they simply another cycle in a dismal downward price spiral?

Get the "Buzz"

As mentioned earlier, you'll want to absorb whatever you can from any possible credible source you can find. The "buzz" about a company usually comes from its customers, its employees, the financial press, or the trade press.

Magazines (paper or web based) like *Design News* can give a lot of information about innovative, new products, particularly in the technology space. Kantar Retail provides a useful industry website, and it publishes trade rags and a free monthly summary of retail activity for the previous month (*www.kantarretail.com*). There are industry journals for almost any industry you might want to follow. Quality free content may not always be easy to find, but you can check with friends in the business or even bite the bullet and pay the price if you want to focus on that industry.

Friends and acquaintances who might be industry insiders may also go to trade shows. These shows are a great way to find out about new products, see how a company is positioning itself and its products, and capture the general buzz. (Which booths are attracting the most attention?) Of course, if you work in an industry yourself, take advantage of these opportunities, too.

I could go on, but you get the idea. Good businesses value their customers and their loyalty, and they pay attention to the experience. They treat people like—well—*customers*. It's not hard to get clues about how and how well they do this. Just put your street shoes on and go check it out. Go be a *marketee*.

Get Into the Habit

- Spend at least a little time, preferably each week, checking out businesses you own or might want to invest in. Do it locally, when you travel, and through friends, family, and acquaintances.
- Pay attention to your own interactions, purchases, and experiences with a company. Could it have been better? Does someone else do it better?
- Look at the level of customer activity, appearance of facilities, and the attitude and helpfulness of employees.
- Check out websites. Give a "plus" to companies with clear, accessible, helpful messages about their products and how they benefit *you*.
- Watch the ads. Are they effective? What are they really telling you?
- Get into the "buzz" network through friends, employers, employees of other companies, and through financial, industry, and trade media.

HABIT 15

Sense the Management Style

Market presence and power, as described in Habits 12–14, can deliver huge intangible benefits to a business and business results. Operating more behind the scenes but just as important—if not more so—is another intangible pillar: company management. Like marketplace factors, you'll have to sense the quality, competence, and trustworthiness of management from a qualitative, sensory assessment—not from formulas, tools, and specific resources.

At the end of the day, what you're really trying to figure out is this: are the senior and most influential managers *achievement* oriented and all in for the shareholders, or are they *power* oriented and all in for themselves? As you try to figure it out, take it against this backdrop: achievement can lead to power, but power rarely leads to achievement.

No corporate manager has given a better example of this than Apple's Steve Jobs. Although difficult to work for at times (especially if you weren't on board with his sense of the customer), his vision, his creation of Apple's culture, his product sense, and his message to the public and to his employees was all about "This is what we can do" and "This is how, Mr. Customer, we will solve your problem." He wasn't just a manager; he was a *leader*.

At Apple, little was said or done about the usual trappings of power, such as promotions, titles, stock options, corporate jets (they didn't have one), and so forth. Managers were there to make products and satisfy customers, not enrich and empower themselves. Jobs created a $500 billion company (and others along the way), but he died with only about 20 percent of the wealth of rival Bill Gates and lived relatively modestly. Gates was a pretty good and fairly visible manager himself, but most of today's corporate big wigs are nameless, faceless entities seemingly wrapped up in title, executive compensation, and perks.

Which kind of management team would you prefer? The answer should be obvious. Is management of a given company a plus, or a minus? Here are a few tips to getting into the habit of sensing a management style:

WHAT WOULD STEVE JOBS DO?

Little wonder that I've used Steve Jobs as an example of leadership excellence, for I wrote a book on the subject. See my *What Would Steve Jobs Do?—How the Steve Jobs Way Can Inspire Anyone to Think Differently and Win* (McGraw-Hill Professional, 2011). What Jobs did should set the standard for anyone examining corporate leadership towards the production of shareholder returns.

Developing the Sense

For those who've been around the block in the corporate world, management excellence may seem to be an insufferable oxymoron. Yet, Warren Buffett views management as an

X-factor that can make all the difference, and he feels he can judge a lot about a company from a short meeting with its senior management.

Evaluating management excellence can be tricky. You don't sit or work with these managers on a daily basis; in fact, much of what they do is deliberately kept secret. Yet, a sensitive antenna can pick up a lot over a period of time. But if you learn about a company in the morning and want to invest that afternoon, appraising management can be pretty difficult.

Solid information about a company's management can be pretty hard to find. Financial portals provide links to the bios and executive compensation of management, but these are really of little value except to detect excessive greed and power. Does management "get it?" For that, you might have to put on your marketing hat, put on your street shoes, look at the achievements in the marketplace, and read and listen to those who may have greater insight—including the managers themselves in conference calls.

Now, what are you looking for?

A Six-Step Leadership Formula

In *What Would Steve Jobs Do?* I laid out a six-step formula designed to guide current and prospective managers towards the excellence and success so obviously created by Jobs and just as obviously *not* apparent in most of corporate America. The management and leadership of a company you own or want to buy can be similarly reviewed against these six steps:

DON'T CONFUSE LEADERSHIP WITH ADMINISTRATION

Some might quip that these six steps really lead to *innovation*, not good overall management. Steve Jobs was most famous as an innovator or more precisely, as a *leader* of innovators (even from day one as he led the more tech-savvy Steve Wozniak towards the early Apple designs). But in today's marketplace, to achieve corporate excellence and growth, especially over a longer term, corporations must innovate and create a culture within which they *can* innovate. The rest is administration, and there are a lot of people out there who can do that for you.

Good management follows all six steps or attributes in balance to achieve good results:

- Customer
- Vision
- Culture
- Product
- Message
- Brand

One at a time:

Customer

Does management "get" the customer? Do they walk a mile in a customer's shoes and create products and experiences that really meet customer needs and solve customer problems? Do they delight the customer and create the sort of excitement and/or loyalty that keeps them coming back? Or do they just fill a lot of shelves with boxes or seats with passengers or tanks with gasoline?

Most companies outsource their market research to, well, market research firms. These firms use proven models to produce commonplace reports that aren't well understood by most managers, if at all—if they even see them. Steve Jobs and other good executives believe in getting their own views of the marketplace through observation, and through direct experience of the company's and competitors' products. John Deere executives, for example, spend time with farmers and in dealerships.

Customer focus can be determined to a degree from company communications. Do communications and advertisements stress how company products benefit customers? Do communications talk about customers and customer "wins," or are they focused on the victories and challenges of the business itself?

When a CEO really takes ownership for what he or she is putting out there, it works, and you can usually tell from the kinds of products and messages put forth. Apple is the clearest example, but there are others such as Ford, John Deere, Chipotle, and others where it seems obvious that someone at the top is looking through the eyes of the customer.

Vision

Customer input and sensitivity does little good unless you can develop a vision around it. Jobs did a couple of things exceptionally well: (1) he developed a holistic vision, one of a complete product that would meet all customer needs in a win-win way (think iPod and iTunes); and (2) he communicated that vision elegantly, simply, and clearly to his people ("a phone, an iPod, and an Internet communications device all in one": the iPhone).

Again, you can see in the marketplace where such complete and forward thinking takes hold. Does a product come with all the supplies and support that you need to make it work (baseline) or really delight (the goal) the customer? Do food products come with good packages and recipes? Hotel rooms come with Wi-Fi and a free soda? Does your Home Depot shopping experience come with helpful floor advisors who really know what they're doing?

Good management teams get the whole product right.

Culture

No vision will go anywhere unless there's a culture in place to make it happen, without error and on time. The marketplace is full of "camels designed by a committee"—products that seem to be the result of risk-adverse, bickering factions within a big company. When insecure management teams suppress risk taking and don't really understand the vision but instead spend their time trying to build and protect their empires, look out below. Or, in the absence of market-focused leadership, when the company seems to be run by the finance department with lots of quality and production short cuts, again, look out below.

Think Ford or GM products in the early 1980s, HP Touchpads, even today's Campbell's Soup cans with inconsistent labeling, some with and some without pop tops, and numerous seemingly overlapping flavors—what's going on inside of Campbell? And what's going on when you can't get a support agent on the line within ten minutes, and then when you finally get to him or her, the agent can't do anything to help?

Good management teams *empower their employees* to do the right thing, independently and without fanfare. They aim their employees toward the customer-directed visions, and they get their products to market on time and with minimal mistakes and rework. Bad ones don't.

Product

You may not see the customer, vision, and culture attributes directly, but you will see (and feel and use) the product. Do the company's products really make sense vis-à-vis what the customers need? Do they leave an impression? Do they support the brand and the brand image? Are they designed, built, packaged, and augmented to do what they're supposed to do?

The quality of a company's physical products or experience tells a lot about the competence and orientation of management.

Message

Does the company have a clear message? Is it articulated to you, the customer? If it isn't, it probably isn't articulated clearly inside the organization, either. Communication is essential in today's rapidly moving business environment, and managers who don't communicate or cloud their communications with jargon and buzzwords simply aren't getting it done. Look and listen to ads and websites and to management conference calls.

And kudos to Mr. Jobs for standing up at Macworld all those years and announcing new products himself—a real and personal commitment to the marketplace and, more subtly, to the employees inside the company. I'm amazed how few other corporate leaders have done this.

Brand

This one is not as much about the brand of the company—the Coca-Cola or John Deere or Tide or Cheer or whichever moniker the company or its products operate under—but it is more about the patterns and behaviors of the management team.

Good management teams are predictable, and are predictable in positive ways. They give clear, simple public explanations for earnings, guidance, and new product plans, with few surprises. They exude competence, and they have candor. They can admit mistakes, and are present in bad times as well as good. (According to Buffett, managers who confess mistakes publicly are "more likely to correct them.") They don't rely on acquisitions for growth or to rescue a slowing or declining business. They don't do reorg after reorg after restructuring, trying to tinker their way to success. They articulate their visions and strategies, and these truly *are* visions and strategies (not just cost cutting). The management teams grow by doing things right, by achieving excellence from within their organizations. That's the key—*achievement.*

Good management teams think and act independently, for the long-term health of the business. They resist the temptation to pour energy and resources into achieving this quarter's results. Buffett calls this approach "avoiding the institutional imperative," which means turning aside the short-term pressures of Wall Street, its analysts, and institutional investors to do what's right for the long-term health of the business. Great management teams have a vision, a mission, and a plan—and they follow them, avoiding distractions. And leadership plays a big part. Unlikely to follow the lead of others, they play to win and to beat the competition, not just to keep up with it.

Good management teams adopt an "achievement" brand, not an arrogant, self-serving "power" brand. Arrogant managers who hide problems think they can solve them all, or, worse yet, think they are invincible and have no problems, are bound for trouble. "Kicking butt" is not always the right answer.

DIALING FOR DOLLARS

You don't—at least in most cases—work for the company you're investing in. So how do you get a chance to listen to what management says and how they say it? How do you pick up the nuances of vision, culture, brand, and so forth? Naturally, it's difficult, and unless you manage a $100 million hedge fund it's obvious you can't just pick up the phone and call. But there is a way for the average investor: conference calls. It's easy and free to listen in on most publicly traded company conference calls on the Internet, through company websites or most financial portals. Transcripts are usually made available on the same sites afterward. The great thing about conference calls: While the initial management message is scripted, the answers to analyst questions aren't. Analysts ask great questions, and you can hear surprisingly honest answers and the tone around them. Someday, maybe they'll appear on YouTube, too, and we can assess the body language.

Get Into the Habit

- Realize from the beginning that understanding management and leadership effectiveness is a "read between the lines" exercise.
- Look for signs of achievement, not signs of power. As Bill Clinton once said, "Power by example, not examples of power."
- Look for signs of customer focus, solid and rational vision, winning culture, winning products, clear, crisp, useful messages, and a solid reputation and management "brand."
- Again remember—you're acquiring a sense. If you think you'd like to work for the company, you're on the right track.

HABIT 16

Look for Signs of Value, Signs of Unvalue

I'll admit that the habits presented so far in Part II have been pretty heavy, sort of a crash MBA in Finance and Marketing all in one. Habits 7 through 15, in fact, will take you a long time to digest and apply as habits. But you'll get there. While it looks like a checklist of 25 specific things to do, *25 Habits* is really a *thought process* about how to evaluate companies to buy and own with some handy flags and tools thrown in for good measure.

Don't despair. You'll get it, eventually.

Meanwhile, I'd like to deploy Habit 16: Look for Signs of Value, Signs of Unvalue as a brief, shorthand list of tangible and intangible character traits to look for in your early analysis of a business. It's sort of like a flight checklist that pilots might use before takeoff in lieu of going through the entire flight manual.

Use this exercise to realistically assess each company for its ten signs of value and unvalue.

Signs of Value

Signs of value are indicators, not definitive judgments, about whether a company is on the right track, just as temperature, humidity, wind speed, wind direction, and cloud cover are all indicators of future weather. They don't dictate the weather with certainty, but they—often together—suggest what might happen.

Tangible Signs of Value

Tangible signs of value relate mainly to financial fundamentals but are driven to a degree by intangibles.

1. *Growing margins*—Are gross, operating, and net profit margins steadily improving? Under any circumstance that's a good sign—it implies market strength, market leadership, pricing power, and greater efficiency.

2. *Producer, not consumer, of capital*—Does the company, as indicated by the Statement of Cash Flows, *produce* more cash, as shown in Cash Flow from Operations, than it consumes in the Cash Flow from Investing (capital expenditures, mostly) and Cash Flow from Financing (increases in debt or equity financing)? Does the company use produced capital to pay dividends and repurchase shares?

3. *Business growing faster than expenses*—Are revenues growing at a faster rate than selling, general, and administrative expenses? If so, that indicates efficiency; if not, it may suggest waste, misspending, or excessive overhead.

4. *Business growing faster than working capital items*—Similarly, are revenues growing faster than inventories and accounts receivable? If not, the company may not be managing its supply chain well. It may not be buying the right stuff or putting it in the right locations. Accounts

receivable outpacing sales suggests that the company is "buying" sales or selling to less creditworthy customers.

5. *Business growing faster than debt*—Again, similar to expenses and working capital, if a company is growing debt faster than it is growing its business, it suggests some waste as debt is being used to purchase unnecessary working capital or physical assets. The company may also be on an acquisition binge. In recent years, some modest debt growth has been taken as prudent because of low interest rates; some companies are even borrowing, as a deliberate strategy, to repurchase shares. But as we all know, debt can't grow forever.

Intangible Signs of Value

Intangible signs of value are really about deciding whether the company has a weak or a strong *moat* around its business to protect it from competition.

1. *Strong brand*—Are the company's brands, or the company brand itself, a strength? Do they deliver up to the level you expect for the brand? Is the brand getting stronger or weaker? Would you (and others) pay a higher price for the brand?

2. *Market or niche leadership*—Does the company control or dominate a niche? Does it have a high share of the market? And thus, can it call the shots on prices?

3. *Customer focus*—Does the company live, breathe, and stand by its customers? Are customer needs really considered, and are they met? Does the company recognize its more valuable customers? Remember, customer focus isn't about doing surveys. It's about really understanding and identifying customers, and treating them well.

4. *Innovation, innovative culture*—Very simply, does the company innovate? And by that, I mean, does it really bring new ideas and products to market or use new processes to deliver products? Or does it simply file a lot of patents, create a lot of jargony web pages, and play a me-too game in the marketplace? Look for signs of true innovation, not just keeping up.

5. *Management a plus, not a drag, on results*—Is management visibly involved in improving the company? Do executives have a clear vision and strategy for where things are going? Or is management instead a lot of cost-cutting, bland, jargony messages, and excuses? Would you want to *work* for this management team?

Signs of Unvalue

Not too surprisingly, signs of unvalue are warning flags—not red flags, but items that might give you some pause about a business. Some, but not all, of these will seem like simple opposites of their corresponding "sign of value." Where I've specifically included such opposites, they might be "orange" flags—a bit stronger than yellow, but still not quite red.

Tangible Signs of Unvalue

1. *Deteriorating margins*—The obvious opposite of growing margins, declining margins suggest declining market power, higher input costs, and/or less operational efficiency. If higher commodity costs are an industry given and affect all industry players evenly (commodities and the food industry or oil in the airline industry), you may

be able to ignore them, especially if it's a cyclical change as opposed to a permanent one.

2. *Deteriorating market share*—This one might be harder to quantify except in industries where market researchers actively report it, like the PC industry. But if a company appears to be losing share, or worse yet, has to continually cut prices to *maintain* share, something's not right.

3. *Can't control cost structure*—Some companies and whole industries can't control most of their costs, and those costs can be highly unpredictable over time. The airline industry is the poster child for this—the carriers have no control over fuel and airport costs and little control over labor and aircraft costs. Just as bad, because of competition they also have little control over prices. Such companies and industries will constantly encounter headwinds.

4. *Inconsistent results*—Earnings and revenues that are up, down, under, and over target from one quarter to the next suggest a company that isn't in control of its environment or may not be in control of itself. That said, some management teams will pull a lot of accounting tricks to achieve consistency. So a little variation is probably good, but if it's big, watch out!

5. *Consumer, not producer, of cash*—Again, one of those "sign of value" opposites but an important one: if a company must continually access the capital markets, that is, offer debt or sell shares to fund operations, be careful. At least be able to understand it, as in the case of a rapidly growing concept company such as CarMax or a new airline.

Intangible Signs of Unvalue

Here one must watch for the footprints of any creature that might undermine a company's market position or financial strength.

1. *Unclear strategy*—If you can't see a clear road forward for a company, take your foot off the accelerator! Scott Bobo and I recently removed Google from the *100 Best Stocks* list because, with all of their acquisitions, we just couldn't see where they were going. We couldn't picture the company five years from now. And, at the risk of repeating from the last habit, cost cutting isn't a strategy unless all you're doing is competing on price.

2. *Unclear message*—When I can't figure out what a company is really trying to tell me about its business, either in its financial reports, conference calls, or on its website or any other management presentation, I tend to stay away. If everything seems like the latest spin compiled from endless buzzwords, or if it seems like excuses, move on.

3. *Acquisition addiction*—Some companies feel so compelled to grow and yet are so locked in by fixed markets, older technologies, and mediocre performance that they buy everything in sight. HP, GE a few years ago, and others couldn't resist the imperative. As a result, they went off the rails managing the businesses they already had. Stick to companies that focus on their existing businesses and try to grow them with innovation and "organic" gains in market share.

4. *Ordinary extraordinaries*—If the company always seems to have some kind of "extraordinary items" to write off in its financial statements, that's a sign of trouble, too. Once in a while is okay; sometimes the company needs to adjust, say, for the cost of an acquisition. But over

and over—these extraordinary items aren't so extraordinary, and should be taken as a cost of doing business, often poorly.

5. *Invisible management*—If nobody's home in the management suite, particularly if they're drawing seven-figure compensation packages, look out. A management team that isn't afraid to stand up to its customer and investors is always better. Know who they are, what they stand for, and what they are likely to say during investor meetings, conference calls, and so forth. After all, they work for you.

These are intended as examples—you may use them or have some of your own, particularly if you're following a specific industry such as retail, where sales per square foot is important, or the movie industry, where the number of academy awards may figure in. Over time, you'll develop your own signs of value and unvalue.

Get Into the Habit

- Create a checklist (or use this one).
- Check it twice.
- Find out who is naughty or nice.
- If Santa never comes, consider adjusting the checklist.

HABIT 17

Do Your Threes—
Three Pros, Three Cons

Here's another simple habit. It's as easy as counting one, two, three.

It's a complex world out there. It's hard to analyze a company. It's hard to compare it to its competitors. It's hard to keep track of the facts, let alone fashion those facts into a meaningful analysis leading to a decision.

We drink from fire hoses all day, every day—from the media, from our friends and families, on the job and in the workplace. New facts, new ideas, and new information are downloaded almost constantly. How do you parse it all down to get what's really meaningful and important?

Researchers have found that people can internalize and digest only three to seven things at a time. Read an article or listen to a speech or presentation, and there had better be only three to seven key points.

I'll take it a step further. I think there should be only three key points. I call it the "principle of threes."

Therein lies Habit 17: Do Your Threes—Three Pros, Three Cons. When you have your facts and impressions together, list the three strongest reasons to buy the investment and three strongest to avoid it.

Three strengths and three weaknesses or three pros and three cons—either way, it's that simple.

Elegant and Simple

Ever listen to a Steve Jobs pitch? To any of his various new product launches at Macworld or some similar venue? Did you notice his technique? Everything is simple. Individual slides often built with only a picture, or at most a picture and a few words.

You may also remember that many of his presentations were built on the principle of threes. First, a series of simple slides, maybe with a picture and one word. Then, summaries and a closing built on three key points.

Unforgettable was the announcement of the first iPhone at Macworld 2007, on January 9, 2007 (*www.youtube.com/ watch?v=Q3W58S29eSE* if you want to follow along). I realize this may appear a little off subject, but it's such a brilliant illustration that I think it's worth sharing. Here's the text of this speech:

> *This is a day I've been looking forward to for two and a half years. Every once in a while, a revolutionary product comes along that changes everything (and first of all, one's very fortunate if you get to work on one of these in your career). Apple has been very fortunate. It has been able to introduce a few of these into the world. In 1984, we introduced the Macintosh. It didn't just change Apple; it changed the whole computer industry [applause]. In 2001, we introduced the first iPod. And it didn't just change the way we all listened to music; it changed the entire music industry. Well, today, we're introducing three revolutionary products of this class.*

The first one is a wide-screen iPod with touch controls [applause]. The second is a revolutionary mobile phone [applause], and the third is a breakthrough Internet communications device [applause].

So, three things.

A wide-screen iPod with touch controls. A revolutionary mobile phone. And a breakthrough Internet communications device.

An iPod, a phone, and an Internet communicator. An iPod, a phone.

Are you getting it? These are not three separate devices. This is one device. And we are calling it the iPhone [applause].

See how elegant and simple this is? He led us into the new product by listing two previous breakthroughs—the Macintosh and the iPod, making us wonder what number three would be. Once there, he took us through the memorable threes of an iPod, a phone, and an Internet communications device."

It didn't take much more than that to get the point across, did it?

Was it memorable? Was it important? You bet.

Three Pros, Three Cons

By now it's probably obvious why I'm suggesting distilling your investment analysis down into three simple, memorable reasons to buy, and three reasons not to buy, a company. This will give you not only a good shorthand to refer back to later if you're looking at a list of companies, but it also forces you to think clearly about what the most important pros and cons are.

Perhaps for Apple it might come out as follows:

Pros

- Worldwide customer acceptance and market leadership
- Extremely high and growing margins
- $80 billion cash on hand

Cons

- Success already priced into $600 shares
- Uncertain where next game-changing innovation will come from
- Uncertain leadership without Steve Jobs

Now you have something you can remember and refer to as you cycle back through your investment analysis. You may—and should—tweak these. You may want to list five or six at first (which would have been easy with Apple, especially on the "pro" side), then distill them further into the threes. If the pros outweigh the cons—well, you know what to do, unless of course there's a better alternative out there.

Get to the Essence

You can also use the principle of threes along the way, prior to getting to that "final" three strengths, three weaknesses analysis. Note in Habit 13, Put on Your Marketing Hat, I illustrated this in the section on SWOT analysis. The SWOT analysis shown in Figure 13.4 gives three strengths, three weaknesses, three opportunities, and three threats. Same idea.

You can also use the principle of threes to break down any fundamental or intangible component. Three strengths and three weaknesses about the balance sheet or statement of cash flows. Three strengths and three weaknesses about the product portfolio or management. It's the same idea.

Get Into the Habit

- Think in terms of threes—three strengths, three weaknesses, or three pros and three cons.
- Write them down, especially for the "final analysis" of a company.
- Amend and adjust as necessary.
- Try it. You'll like it. It works.

Buy with a Margin of Safety

You've been examining a business. Is it a good business? Is it a business you want to buy?

Perhaps you've made a "yes" decision; you want to own it. That's nice; it's always good to know what you want. But there's one more small little detail, isn't there?

Indeed—just as there is in any other buying decision. What is the *price?* Just how much of your hard-earned cash (capital) will you have to lay out to buy the thing? Is it worth it?

Sure, there are lots of great businesses out there. We'd all like to own Apple—it's a great business. But do we want to own it at today's price? That's the tough decision.

This habit is about deciding if the price is right and about giving yourself a margin of safety in case you're wrong.

What a Business is Worth—In Theory, Anyway

Scholars and graduate students of finance have written mountains of research papers on the valuation of businesses. While there is a lot of merit to the "discounted cash flow" model and other such concepts, I propose a simpler way to think about a business—which at the end of the day isn't too far off the "DCF" approach anyway.

Here goes: the value of a business is simply the total cash you'll receive from the company during your time of ownership—nothing more, nothing less.

Now, that cash can come in several forms:

- *Dividends*—These are cash payments you'd receive regularly or irregularly from the business, not unlike an owner's withdrawal from a small independently owned business.
- *Share repurchases*—When a company goes to the market to repurchase shares, that would make your shares—in theory, at least—more valuable.
- *Final sale*—If the business is sold to another business, you'll receive cash from that transaction. The value at the time of the sale should reflect any earnings that are retained in the business (as opposed to being paid to you in dividends). So the earnings, as reported, represent an eventual cash flow if all goes well and it isn't lost. Selling your stock is like selling the business and should be looked at the same way.

The sum total of these three activities, over time, is what you, the owner, will get out of a business—nothing more, nothing less. The only other factor to consider is timing—a large cash flow today is worth more than the same cash flow twenty years from now. That's where the "discounted" in the DCF model comes in. The math is beyond scope here, but the concept is important.

Simply, will you get enough cash *out* of the business, now and in the future, to justify your investment?

Navigating Those P-to-Something Ratios

Now that we've gotten the "theoretical" thing out of the way, what price should you pay for a share of stock? Reaching back to theory, it will be something connected to the amount of cash you expect to receive over time for your ownership of that share of stock.

Estimating cash flows over a period of time can be very difficult for an investor. (It's hard enough for the managers directly involved with the business!) So investors and financial analysts use a shorthand based on ratios. Many of these ratios, like the Price-to-Earnings (P/E) are commonly presented and discussed as part of a standard information matrix about a stock on a financial portal or elsewhere.

- *Price/Earnings Ratio.* "P/E" is simply the current price of the stock divided by earnings per share for the trailing twelve months. It is sometimes referred to as the "trailing" P/E ratio, while a "forward" P/E ratio compares price to projected per-share earnings over the next twelve months. It is an approximation of the *long-term* cash return potential of the business—even though in the short term, most of this return is kept as retained earnings instead of being returned as cash. What "should" a P/E be? The answer is complex. Different P/E standards apply to different industries, depending on the industry's growth potential, stability, strength of cash flow, and myriad other factors. P/E is also driven by the returns available on alternative investments, thus will be higher when fixed returns, or interest rates are low. The next metric makes more sense of this:
- *Earnings Yield.* "EY" is simply the reciprocal of P/E and represents the effective yield of the investment. A stock with a P/E ratio of 25 has an earnings yield of 4

percent (1/25), and thus can be compared with other investments, including relatively risk-free interest bearing investments. If you're investing in a stock with a P/E of 25, the return should be better than the alternative yields available. But there's yet *another* factor: growth.

- *Price-to-Earnings-to-Growth.* The Price-to-Earnings-to-Growth, or "PEG" ratio, normalizes P/E ratios to account for growth; that is, a stock with a P/E of 25 and an annual earnings growth rate of 25 percent has a PEG of 1, much better than another stock with a P/E of 25 and a more meager earnings growth rate of 5 percent; that PEG is 5. Recall the earlier cash-flow discussion—companies with sustainable growth have higher long-term cash returns and thus greater value. Paying 25 times current earnings may be justified with a high projected growth rate. Generally, stocks with a PEG of around 1, or less, are attractively priced, and those over 3 are overpriced.

- *Price-to-Cash-Flow.* Recalling that cash flow, especially over the long term, may be a better indicator of true business activity, some analysts look at price-to-cash-flow as an alternative to P/E. Some dig further to look at price-to-free-cash-flow, that is, cash flow available after capital investments.

- *Price-to-Sales.* "P/S" is a quick indicator of price acceptability. It is the ratio of price to per-share revenues or sales, sometimes also calculated as "market capitalization" (price of shares times number of shares outstanding) divided by total revenues. As an individual buying a small business, you would hesitate to pay three or four times annual sales for a business; ideally it would be one or less. This is also true for investments, although growth rates and profit margins must be considered.

- *Price-to-Book.* "P/B" is share price divided by the accounting book value, or owner's equity, per share. Unfortunately, as discussed way back in Habit 10: Value Thy Fundamentals, the book value may not reflect reality, so this measure is relatively less useful for most industries. It does have merit in financial services and similar industries, where most of the assets are cash and securities.

Summing up, valuation ratios are handy ways to gauge not the success but the *price* of a business. They're particularly useful in comparing it to other businesses. Ratios help make sense of the financials and the stock price. You'll find most key ratios on financial portal pages, often on a "key statistics" page or something similar.

LET THE RATIO ANALYST BEWARE

All financial analysts, amateur or professional, must avoid the temptation to use ratios and other financial analysis tools without thinking about the underlying numbers. If a company takes a one-time charge for a restructuring or layoff, the P/E will be distorted by the earnings "hit." So it helps to examine the underlying financials, including the company's own discussion, before taking the analysis as gospel. That said, a company that has these "special" occurrences all the time (and some companies do) should be judged accordingly.

If You Had $50 Billion . . .

Ratios, cash flow, math, numbers—it may be a bit overwhelming, especially for you part-time investor/business owners who have a full-time job or something else important to do throughout the day. It can get pretty tedious and dry even if you do have the time.

One test I perform regularly when considering an investment is to simply pretend I'm buying the business—the whole business. Now, is this really a surprise after reading Habit 7: Buy Like You're Buying a Business?

Here's how you do it. Simply take the "market cap"—which stands for market capitalization and is the current share price times all share outstanding. You'll get a number—a big number—a number that is routinely reported in most financial portals as "market cap" or something similar.

The market cap is the total value of a company as perceived by the *market*. The "market" is the whole of the investment community buying and selling a stock, and thus setting price at a particular level through the aggregate of all their decisions.

So you get a number, a number like $41 billion for Starbucks or $38 billion for HP or $40 billion for Costco or $17 billion for Kellogg's or $169 billion for Coca-Cola, or a whopping $500 billion for Apple (the biggest one out there).

If you had the dough, would you buy one of these businesses? Would you buy Starbucks for $41 billion? Would you rather buy Starbucks, HP, or Costco at that price? Would you rather buy Coca-Cola or the three businesses just mentioned, plus another of that size thrown in for good measure? Or how about buying Kellogg's and keeping $25 billion or so dry for the next idea?

And is the market *right* about the valuation it gives the company? As Warren Buffett would tell you, the market is often wrong.

While it's a bit of a fantasy game, it's fun to play, and it helps you ferret out which companies you'd really like to own *at a given price*. That tells you a lot about whether you'd really like to own *a few shares* of that company.

Providing the Margin of Safety

Valuation is far from an exact science. If it were precise, we'd buy a stock when the P/E fell below 12, sell it when it rose above 12, and laugh all the way to the bank. There'd be nothing to this, right?

The fact is, valuation is extremely imprecise, and price, the actual price tag put on a stock by the aggregate investment community, is even *less* precise. Value is uncertain, and price is even more uncertain because thousands of parties out there have a different view of what that value is.

As an investor, you aren't going to beat this rap completely. You may have a better, more rational approach to valuing a business than the next guy or gal, and you may have a better sense of what to pay than the next investor. That's great, but you'll never be exactly right. It's like predicting the weather— lots of observations, lots of data, lots of models, and lots of interpretation. But it still rains on your picnic.

What do you do as an investor? You look for a margin of safety. This idea was pioneered back in the beginning of value-oriented investing—way back in the 1930s, by Benjamin Graham, who just happened to become Buffett's teacher. You look at the company, you decide what price range is right, and then you look for an even lower entry point—just in case you're wrong.

So if you decide that Starbucks is a good value at $41 billion, or $53 per share, step back and wait—maybe you can pick it up for $47 or so, a 10 percent discount. That 10 percent gives you a margin of safety in case you're wrong. It isn't foolproof, but it will help a lot over time.

Get Into the Habit

- Look at a business value as the sum of *all* future cash flows.
- Look at the ratios. Use them as a guide to future returns and to compare alternatives.
- Pretend you're buying the whole business—*still* want to buy it?
- Give yourself an extra margin of safety, by buying at a price dip, just in case.

PART III

OWN FOR SUCCESS: GETTING THE MOST OUT OF YOUR PORTFOLIO

Once you buy a stock or some other investment, are you done? Hardly. If you bought the entire business, you'd have to stay in touch with how well it's doing, manage it to get the most out of it, and sell it if performance slips or if there was something else better to buy.

The seven habits of Part III help you get the most out of your ownership and especially with making those oh-so-difficult selling decisions.

Buy Smart—
When You Decide to Buy

You've twisted and turned, heaved and sighed, pondered and stressed over whether to acquire business XYZ. You've followed all the Part II habits closely (of course) to come to your decision: Yes, you want to own XYZ. A few shares of it anyway. It's a good business, and you want to invest some of your precious hard-earned capital to get on board with its current and future prospects—at the current price or something close—before the train leaves the station.

Now what?

This is where many a patient investor has lost his or her head. They try to catch the low price for the week, the month, or the year. Maybe it's about saving a little money; maybe it's about bragging rights; I don't know. It's like buying a quality product in a regular store. You know that you need it. You're going to buy it anyway, and you're going to own it for a while. So why spend weeks waiting for it to go on sale to save a few percent? Why drive all over town, using gas, to save a few pennies per gallon on gas?

Yet, people do it all the time.

This habit is about not just investing smart, but *buying* smart. It's about paying some attention to price behavior to try for a good entry point, but no waiting forever. It's about *not* waiting too long or playing games with market makers and dealers who sell the stock just to save a few cents. Finally, we'll discuss an advanced topic—covered puts—that allows you to turn a firm buy decision into current cash income.

Watch—For a While, Anyway

You finish your analysis, and the decision is, yes—I want to own company XYZ. Now what? You can log on to your online broker and buy. That's probably okay, for if you're buying for the long term, who cares about today's up-and-down twitter in the price?

That's generally the *modus operandi* you should be in. You want to own an investment for five, seven, ten, twenty years—is a short term 1 percent premium you're asked to pay because the market is strong today really that important? In the grand scheme of things, no, but . . .

I like to watch price movement just a bit before I buy, as well as look at the recent past with a chart. Why? Well, for me, it is one last gut check into the health of a company, and it is an opportunity to maybe find a better entry point, especially on a really good business that might be going steadily higher in the long run. I'm not going to look at every gas station in town, but I may look at one or two others.

I do like to assess the short-term trend, also. If it is decidedly weak, it may reflect a flaw in my analysis, especially if most of the market is going sideways or higher. Moreover, as much as I'd like to believe in perfect information—that is, that everyone in the market has the same information at their fingertips—I know this is not the case. If the company is having a period of slowing sales, increased input costs, or some other factor that might affect the business results, there are people closer to the situation than I who probably know. That's a fact of life. The trick, of course, is to try to figure out the source of malaise, and to decide if it affects the business in the long term. If not, you've probably just stumbled onto another buying opportunity.

Likewise, if the short-term trend is hot, you might wait a few days for it to cool. Even the hottest stocks will usually pull back when the markets pull back. I'm in the habit of always buying on a "down" day; it just increases my chances of not paying too much for a stock, and there are enough down days that you usually don't have to wait too long.

The risk, again, is that you *do* wait too long, and the train leaves the station without you. It's better to get on board slightly higher than you really want to pay than to chase the train down the tracks into oblivion.

Obviously there is no science to this—really, it is an art acquired from experience. Be observant, and be patient—but not *too* patient If you've made the right business decision, go for it.

No Limits to your Buying

Stockbrokers and most investing literature extol the virtues of special order types you can use when buying or selling a stock. These order types allow you to specify a price and/or a condition upon which the order will execute or become active in the marketplace.

The most popular of such order types is the *limit* order. This specifies a price at which you want to buy or sell a security. It can only be executed if someone on the other side of the market—a dealer or another investor or trader—agrees to that price. "Buy Intel, 100 shares, limit $27.50, good for the day" is a good example of how such an order might read.

(You don't type out these instructions, the brokerage website prompts the entries.) That means you're willing to pay exactly $27.50, not a penny more, for your 100 shares of Intel, and that intention (known as a *bid* in the market) will be cancelled if not executed during that trading day.

Nice to have, and these orders have their place—for traders. Traders make their living buying and selling, buying and selling, making a few cents or a buck or two, back and forth, through the day, week, or even longer periods. But they're simply trading the securities for short-term gains; they're not investing; they don't care that much about the *business* or their ownership thereof. They're buying and selling stocks, not businesses. There's nothing wrong with that; it just isn't really investing.

Limit orders make a lot of sense—for traders. Traders need to control their entry and exit prices to assure their short-term gains. Traders act like dealers in an antiques marketplace—they look for good deals, they buy and try to sell as soon as possible at a higher price. To do that, they need to be able to buy and sell at a set price.

As an investor, you don't need to do that. Who cares if you pay $27.50 or $27.51 for Intel, if you plan to own it for ten years? A market order just says, "buy"; then the brokerage platform goes to the market to find the best price available. So, as a true value oriented, own-the-business investor, you should use market orders.

Buying—Early and Often

You're a busy investor, too busy to spend a lot of time constantly analyzing the markets and businesses you own. You're bringing in good income from your day job. How can you make sure your money gets invested in the best way possible without spending all weekend, every weekend, doing the sort of analysis we covered in Part II?

I believe that prudent investors should believe in themselves and believe in their picks, and stick with them. And keep investing in them. Not that you don't keep tabs—I'll cover that later. But as your investment capital flows in, I believe in deploying it fairly regularly into your investments. That is, buy a few more shares at regular, perhaps monthly, intervals, to build your position. This assumes, of course, that you're well enough diversified (five to seven stocks or funds; see Habit 4) and don't need to add any new holdings.

Investment professionals and talk show hosts cite the advantages of so-called "dollar cost averaging," or DCA. Often they make it sound like rocket science, but it's not that complicated. Here's how it works: You set aside a consistent amount to invest, say, $5,000 per quarter. You allocate this investment across the portfolio, buying X shares of Company A, Y shares of Company B, etc.—whatever is dictated by the current price. (With the high brokerage commissions of yesteryear this used to be a bad idea, but with today's trading costs in the $10 range per trade, it's probably okay).

The wisdom of this approach, aside from a steady and disciplined savings approach, is that you buy *more* shares of Company A when the stock is cheap, *fewer* when it is expensive. Over time, that will lower the average price basis for *all* the shares you own, and you'll end up making more money.

See? You can be a financial talk show host, too.

Advanced Topic: Selling Puts to Buy

Those of you who are scared of things that sound scary, like *options* and *derivatives*, can stop here and go on to the next habit.

For the rest of you curious and intrepid investors, here's a technique to turn your buying intentions into a little current cash income. I'll discuss the "mainline" application of options to generate income *on what you already own* in Habit 22—Pay Yourself. This habit is about generating income *on what you've decided to buy.*

Options are market-traded securities designed to allow an investor (or trader) to buy or sell the *right* to buy or sell a security at a fixed, determined price *("strike price")*, at or before a fixed, predetermined future date (*"expiration date"*). That right is worth money and thus is bought or sold as a separate security, and the price of that security is known as a *premium.* The buyer of an option pays the premium; the seller collects it.

There are two types of options. An option to buy a security at a strike price by a certain expiration date is called a *call*; an option to sell a security at a strike price by a certain date is called a *put.* An investor who wanted to bet on a stock going up would buy a call, because the call would increase in value as a stock approached, and especially as it exceeded, the strike price. An investor who wanted to bet on a stock going *down* would buy a put, giving him the right to *sell* the stock at a fixed price, which could come in handy if the stock dropped below that fixed price.

So an investor "bullish" on Intel (current price $27.50) might buy September 28 calls (current month May) and pay, say, $1 for them. If the stock is still at $27.50 in September at the expiration date, the calls will be worthless. But in May they have a value, because who knows—the stock could go to $32 by September. Investors and traders pay the premium to get this possibility. The seller of the call option, presumably who owns the Intel shares, wants to earn the $1 premium, and hopes the stock closes at $27.99 on the expiration date, so that he can keep the shares.

Now let's turn this around to the sell side and talk about *puts*. An investor someplace out there in the market owns 100 shares (that's the contract minimum—1 option contract is for 100 shares) and is worried that Intel might go down. So he buys a September $27 put, giving him the right to sell at $27 by the expiration date. Of course, he comes out ahead if the stock drops below $27. The investor is effectively buying insurance for that part of his or her portfolio.

Now we get to how you can make a few short-term bucks on your buying decision. You've decided to buy Intel, and you think that $27.50 is a fair price. But you're a patient investor and are in no hurry. You have $2,750 in cash sitting in your brokerage account. Here's what you can do: Instead of buying the shares, consider selling the September $27 put to that other investor. (This is easier to do than it sounds; your broker likely has easy option trading platforms—just ask.) So you collect the $1 premium ($100) for essentially doing nothing. If the stock drops to $26, you'll end up owning the stock at $27 (the other investor will exercise his or her option to sell it to you). But hey—you had already decided that owning at $27.50 was okay.

Instead of buying right away, you can sell puts to bring in some current cash. You will end up keeping the cash, and you may end up owning the shares at a price you already decided is okay.

Got it? Do a couple of practice laps before competing in the big race.

Get Into the Habit

- Be patient. Watch the stock for a few days at least before jumping in.
- Buy when you decide to buy; use market orders; don't play games to try to save a few cents.
- Add to your investments regularly; take advantage of dollar cost averaging.
- If so inclined, sell *put* options to earn a little more from your buying decisions.

HABIT 20

Keep Your Finger on the Pulse

As we switch gears from choosing and buying companies to actually owning them, you'll find a lot of similarities between the habits you might deploy to *buy* and the habits you might deploy to *own*. When you buy a company, you have expectations, and those expectations are set according to your analysis of the company.

Before you buy a company, you dig in to first figure out whether the company can meet your expectations during the course of your ownership. You learn about the company, you assess its strengths and weaknesses, and you decide if it's a good business to own.

When you own the business, you go through a similar process, except that you're making sure that it continues to meet your expectations. Since you own shares but aren't a manager, there's little you can do to change the course. But there's a lot you can do to know what the course is and how well the company is staying on it.

In this habit, you'll learn to watch your company as any absentee business owner might. Check the stock price and news stories at least once a week; read up on not just the company but also the industry. Read earnings announcements, attend investor conference calls, etc.

The Weekly Review

I'll keep this simple. At minimum, you should check your investments at least once a week. Daily is probably better, but not all of us have the time or are interested.

Check the stock price (and it's always handy to remember the price you bought it at). Check for recent news stories. The best way to do this is usually online through one of the various financial portals; Google Finance and Yahoo!Finance are among the best, but many brokerage sites offer the same features. Financial newspapers like the *Wall Street Journal* and *New York Times* business section give you an index of stories by company. With today's "smart" devices, there are a lot of ways to stay on top of news stories about a company.

Best is to set aside some time early in the morning, late at night, or on a weekend to surf through the stories that might affect your companies. Make it regular. You may also want to scan through company websites to get a "what's new" refresh—maybe not every company you own every week, but at least once in a while.

The idea is to "drip irrigate" your knowledge base.

The Quarterly Financial Report

When your businesses announce their quarterly earnings, it's a good time to pay attention. Most companies publish their announcement date well in advance. Good, informative earnings releases not only give the past financials but some projections of future financials and the key fundamentals that drive them, such as higher profit margins and cash flow; quarterly reports also indicate some intangibles such as new innovations, major marketplace wins, and so forth. Useful, clearly explained information and a good balance between tangible and intangible subjects usually suggests a competent, transparent management team and a good story. If you read an earnings announcement and don't know what they're talking about—*it might not be you*. There may be a reason why things aren't being made clear.

Once again, conference calls are an excellent way to not only pick up the facts but also the nuance and tone, and the sense of past, present, and future success or failure that might come from the management team. There will be a scripted presentation of the financials—which, of course, as scripted material, can be set up to spin almost anything. Beyond that, analyst questions and management's answers to those questions can be very revealing, although some analysts go too far to play "stump the chump," picking on some distant corner nuance that management can't be reasonably expected to explain.

Listen in, and you'll pick up a lot from conference calls. It's probably your best chance to hear from your company's managers.

The Personal Experience

Habit 14: Put on Your Street Shoes is important during ownership as well as during your initial consideration for purchase. Why? Because you should see several things for yourself whether:

- The *company* and its products are still resonating with customers. Are people still excited about Apple products and Starbucks coffee?

- The *experience* still lives up to expectations. Are there new inhibitors on the scene, like long lines to buy, dirty facilities, etc. Remember, it's not just the product, it's the experience, and the experience should live up to and strengthen the brand.
- The *"buzz"* is still there. Are people still talking about Apple products and Starbucks coffee? Is it in a positive light? Or are they annoyed at high prices, lousy service, and so forth
- The *innovation* is on track. Are the new models at car dealers really new? Are there signs of innovation and steps towards market leadership? How do they look and feel to you? Are they catching the eyes of others? What are the dealership people saying about them? What have you seen in the media?

Heck, you can put on street shoes and wander around looking for all of these things—or you can simply buy the product! A few bucks spent here and there at a company you own doesn't hurt every once in a while. I do it a lot. Ask yourself, as you experience the product, would you still want to own the company? Obviously, if the company makes military fighters, this is impractical. But if you fly commercially and own Boeing stock, ask yourself whether getting on that airplane is still a positive experience.

What Is the Competition Doing?

Smart businesspeople don't operate in a vacuum. Instead, they always have one eye open toward the competition. What is the competition doing? What products are they selling? What new products do they have? Are they getting the buzz, the word of mouth, the press coverage? Are you? How are they marketing their products? What are some key operational characteristics that make their business successful, or that inhibit their business? And, are your company's competitive advantages and competencies still in place? Are they still as strong as they were? As an investor, you should keep at least a corner of your eye on the competitors in your industry. What, and how, are they doing? Are they winning in the marketplace? Are they making more money than your company is? Or is your company still in front and/or gaining momentum?

If you own Starbucks, walk into a Peet's or a Caribou Coffee outlet. Is the experience better or worse? Is it busier or less busy? Is it cleaner or dirtier? Is the coffee better or worse? Such appraisals can tell as much, if not more, than what's offered in the next quarterly financial report.

HAVE LUNCH WITH YOUR SMART FRIENDS

As much time as I spend on stocks, I know I can't keep up with everything going on in an industry, particularly a complex, rapidly changing industry such as most of high tech. I suggest making friends in the industry or close to it if possible (like an electronics retailer, to learn about the computer industry), and spending some quality time once in a while. Have a lunch, and pick your acquaintance's brains for the latest customer, product, and business trends. Sense the spirit, sense the mood, sense the excitement. If all they do is complain about how complex and inefficient their business is, how everything's "in the toilet," look out below.

It'll cost you a lunch, but that's a small price to pay for good business information. And, hopefully, you'll enjoy the lunch. But remember, it's just one of many, many data points. *Bon appetit!*

Get Into the Habit

- Make regular time to scan the news, get quotes, and check the progress of companies you own.
- Observe quarterly financial reports carefully and listen to the conference calls.
- Put your street shoes on. Wander around, sense the business, sense the customers, and make sure the business is still on track.
- Keep tabs on the competition.
- Keep in touch with industry experts.

React, But Don't Overreact, to News

*"Company XYZ reports that its chief financial officer
has left the company to pursue other interests."*

*"Company XYZ announces that its chief financial
officer spent two weeks last summer as a volunteer for
Habitat for Humanity."*

*"The chief financial officer of company XYZ now
gives guidance that earnings will be 20 percent lower
for the current quarter."*

Such headlines as these three might be something you see
in the course of regular news "grazing." Some headlines are
really relevant and suggest a lot about the shape of the business itself; others, while important to a few individuals or the
eyeball-seeking news organizations that put them out there,
say little about the health or course of a business.

The "habit" presented here centers on helping you
react properly—but not overreact—to news items. Many an
investor has lost his or her head, selling on the day of a bad
announcement—where institutions react almost instinctively
(sometimes through complex computer algorithms with no
human interaction at all) to a big, bad news story. A stock

that traded 5 million shares a day suddenly trades 100 million, as panicked investors (and computers) dump shares out the window. The stock price may crater 20, 30, even 50 percent. Is this the right time to sell? In my experience, almost never, especially for the patient, long-term investor. Outside of mergers and acquisitions, rarely has a single day's announcement changed the course of a business entirely.

You should be concerned if bad news surfaces (or if the markets sour), but avoid selling the day of the news; let things settle out. You should always try to distinguish between a short-term bad news blip and fundamental changes in the business.

In short—take a deep breath. Separate the news from the noise.

Here are some common types of news, and how, in general, to react to them:

Bad Quarterly Earnings News

Look especially at what *drove* the change—shrinking margins, increased costs, or declining volumes. Try to discern whether these changes are one-time blips or permanent. Is the problem controllable (that is, is it internal to the business?), or is it a product of the business environment? Does it affect your company? Or all companies in the business?

Look at trends where possible. Listen to what management has to say. As usual, a good test is to think of what you would do if you owned the business yourself, and your management team came to you with such a results report. How would you react? Also, recognize that a stock usually ramps up a bit prior to an announcement, in anticipation of what's *possible* (even if not probable), so a bad market performance could simply be an unwinding of these gains.

Guidance Changes

Closely related to earnings announcements are changes in earnings or revenue guidance, usually for the upcoming quarter or annual period. These announcements, especially the annual guidance announcements, can tell a lot about the health of the business, perhaps more since they are forward rather than backward looking. Again, you should look for factors that *drove* the change, whether they are internal or external, and, in sum, whether the business itself has changed as a consequence.

Executive Departures

This one's a bit tricky. Workers leave companies for all sorts of reasons, and important "C-level" executives (CEO, CFO, COO, CMO, CIO, etc.) are no different. Executives can leave for personal reasons or, when they're at the top of their game, to "pursue other interests." But a departure in one of these key posts can be at least a yellow flag that something is wrong in the company—or with the function that executive is leading. A CFO (chief financial officer) departure, for example, could be a signal that the company's finances are suspect, either because of financial health or compliance issues.

The best course of action, therefore, is to see what announcements follow and do some poking around in the area of the departed officer. If debt levels, debt service, inventories, receivables, and writeoffs all appear reasonable, then it's more likely that the officer really *did* leave for personal reasons. In any event, news items like this should have you watching more closely.

Acquisitions and Acquisition Rumors

If your company is the acquirer, that can send the stock price lower, as investors flee the cost and complexity of the acquisition. The trick here is to really understand how the acquisition plays into the existing business; whether the company is being bought for the sake of buying growth or because it synergizes with and improves the business. That merits closer study.

Of course, if your company is the *acquiree*, it's a different matter. You'll have to make a decision—as any business owner would—about whether to take the cash or keep the business.

New Product Announcements

Some companies make a bigger deal about announcing new products than others. Apple leads the way in this regard, but how much interest is there in the latest computer chip or flavor of cereal or a new store opening in Kankakee, Illinois? It varies. Sharp investors read these announcements but look more for signs of innovation and emerging market leadership than anything in the announcements themselves. By the way, I also take a dim view of close-vested companies than never announce *anything*—innovation and success shouldn't always be kept a secret, should they?

New Customer Announcements

Similarly, a lot of companies, especially tech companies, announce new customers and customer wins. "*XYZ Technologies announces the sale of 2,000 workstations to the Defense Department,*" or some such. Like product announcements, a lot of these announcements are basic PR and don't say much about the real success and health of the business.

Restructuring Announcements

Companies will, from time to time, hit the wires with large layoff and restructuring announcements. Sometimes they're a surprise, and sometimes they're long anticipated and factored into the stock price already. The key things you should ask about restructurings are:

- Does the restructuring indicate a fundamental change in the business, or is it more of a housecleaning or adjustment, possibly related to an acquisition or other one-time event?
- Are the "one-time" restructurings seemingly ongoing? Do they signal a perpetual housecleaning, reflect bad business trends, indicate sloppy management, etc. One way to tell is if you observe a pro forma earnings announcement excluding "extraordinary expenses" alongside a "GAAP" (Generally Accepted Accounting Principles) set of statements in a company's quarterly reports. Too much focus on non-GAAP reporting suggests that management may be trying to make things look better than they really are.

Like the other news items on this list, this one will usually bear further investigation.

Brokerage Recommendation Changes

Brokers such as Goldman Sachs, JPMorgan Chase, Jefferies & Co., and a host of other, smaller firms put out their recommendations to buy, sell, or hold, or their own nomenclature for any of the three.

Over the years I have found brokerage recommendation changes to be untimely and fairly uninformative—with companies being downgraded to "sell" after losing half their value, not before. I also find them to be often done in herd mentality; that is, they tend to follow each other and *not* to give fresh perspective. That all said, the markets are still dominated by institutional players, and institutional players tend to listen to these recommendations. What I recommend you do is try to find some kind of report online (maybe through your own broker, or through your financial portal) with a more thorough write-up explaining the change and its rationale. Read the rationale to see if it changes your mind about the business, and act accordingly.

Incidentally, I put much more value in the analysis done by *Value Line* than I do in most analysis at brokerages. The editors at *Value Line* explain their assumptions, and there are no biases triggered by customer relationships with large institutional investors or the companies themselves that are being rated.

Get Into the Habit

- Stop, look, and listen to new news announcements. Don't ignore them.
- React by digging further.
- Think of yourself as the owner.
- Don't overreact with an ill-considered sell (or buy) reflex.

HABIT 22

Pay Yourself

I like to be paid. Don't you?

This gets back to the real reason, the core essential reason, to invest. You want a return. And what is the true value of ownership of any business? If you've been reading along, way back in Habit 18: Buy with a Margin of Safety you learned that the value of a business is the sum value of all cash you will receive from it in the short and long term. For most businesses, that refers to the earnings generated by that company and paid to you in the form of owner's withdrawals (for a small business) or dividends (from shares in a large corporation) and the value you'd receive from the eventual sale of the business or its shares.

So with any investment, you have a choice. Pick an investment that pays more cash now and in the short-term future, or an investment that retains all of its earnings, pays no dividends, and pays cash to you when you sell. The earnings—at least in theory—will accrue to the value of the business when you sell.

That seems like an easy choice because it really makes no difference in the long run. Pay me now or pay me later. But there's one more little fly in the ointment that you need to consider. If you wait for the "later" payout, what's the guarantee that it's going to happen? None. In the amount that you expect? None. The longer you have to wait for that eventual cash payout, the more things that can get in the way.

As the old expression goes, a bird in hand is worth two in the bush. Similarly, a dollar of cash in hand today may well be worth two in the bush to claim twenty years down the road.

As a prudent investor, I think you should be looking for at least a few birds in hand. You should look to get at least some of your cash return now and in the short term to guarantee that you'll get some at all. Heck, it makes for some nice spending money (or reinvesting money) too.

With that in mind, I prefer companies that pay at least *some* dividends. To me, that represents management's dedication to the proposition of sharing some of its wealth with you *now*, and paying you some current return for the use of your hard-earned capital. You may choose a few companies such as Google, Apple (until 2012), and others that feel they can reinvest earnings better than you can (your call as to whether that's true), but as a rule I tend to be very careful with these kinds of companies; you should too. Perception may not be reality.

Habit 22: Pay Yourself is about getting some current cash out of your investments. The easiest, probably the best and most straightforward way to do this is through dividends. But I'll share a couple of other techniques to keep in mind: short-term rotational plays and selling covered call options.

Give Yourself a Paycheck

To repeat, I like dividend-paying stocks. There are dozens of solid companies out there that not only pay a decent yield, but also have decent growth prospects and are large enough and strong enough to be safe. Over time, the dividend should grow, and the share price should, too.

In the 2013 timeframe, a dividend yield ranging in the 2 to 4 percent range is very good. Government bonds are yielding less than 2 percent, and if you pick a company such as Johnson & Johnson or something similar, the yield is probably *almost* as safe. *Almost*, I say, for any company can cut any dividend at any time for any reason, whereas at least thus far, U.S. Government security interest payments are virtually guaranteed. But still you're getting a higher yield with the stock, almost twice as high, and you have growth prospects. With a bond, you have absolutely zero growth prospects, and if you aren't willing to hold the bond until maturity, the bond can decline in value too if interest rates go up. Further, at least for now, dividends get a preferential tax treatment, with a 15 percent cap on the Federal income tax rates for most of us. Bond interest is taxed at—well—whatever your marginal tax rate is.

So higher yield, dividend growth, share price growth, favorable tax treatment, and an opportunity to participate in the growth in the economy versus a low yield and no growth prospects—which would you rather have?

Now, as I said, dividends are by no means guaranteed by the businesses that pay them. Back in 2007, banks were making money hand over fist, and the dividends paid by those banks were attractive. They seemed to have all the attributes of cash flow, growth, and safety that investors would look for. We all know the rest of that story. Dividends were cut, to zero in many cases, and now banks must seek regulatory approval to raise those dividends; very few have returned to their 2007 levels. That was a rather extreme example, but it supports the notion of "let the dividend investor beware."

With all of this in mind, I'll share twenty stocks that, as of 2013, should have solid prospects, given a realistic future and given that you resist the temptation to put all of your eggs in one basket. This list of "yield stars" comes directly from my sister book *The 100 Best Stocks to Buy in 2013*.

TABLE 22.1: YIELD STARS

Top-20 Dividend Paying Stocks From *The 100 Best Stocks to Buy in 2013*

Company	Symbol	Dividend	Yield %	Dividend raises, past 10 years
Suburban Propane	SPH	$3.41	7.8%	10
Total S.A.	TOT	$2.61	6.2%	5
AT&T	T	$1.76	5.7%	9
Cincinnati Financial	CINF	$1.61	5.7%	10
Verizon	VZ	$2.00	5.5%	6
Otter Tail Corporation	OTTR	$1.19	5.4%	5
Duke Energy	DUK	$1.00	4.8%	6
Southern Company	SO	$1.96	4.3%	10
PayChex	PAYX	$1.28	4.2%	8
Waste Management	WM	$1.42	4.2%	8
Dominion Energy	D	$2.11	4.1%	8
Kimberly-Clark	KMB	$2.96	4.0%	10
Johnson & Johnson	JNJ	$2.44	3.8%	10
NextEra Energy	NEE	$2.40	3.8%	10
ConocoPhillips	COP	$2.64	3.7%	10
Heinz	HNZ	$1.92	3.6%	8
Molex	MOLX	$0.80	3.6%	10
Nucor Corp.	NUE	$1.46	3.6%	8
Sysco	SYY	$1.08	3.6%	10
Campbell's Soup	CPB	$1.16	3.5%	9

This list provides twenty ways for you to pay yourself and to enjoy some gains in the future. There are others easily found with stock screeners or by simply parsing the holdings of high-yield stock funds or ETFs, like the iShares Dow Jones Select Dividend Index Fund (symbol: DVY).

Give Yourself a Raise

We all like a steady paycheck, right? But isn't it better if that paycheck comes with an occasional raise? Maybe a regular raise? There's a lot of power in that idea. If you buy a company that pays, say, 3 percent today, and it raises its dividend 10 percent a year, then guess what? That dividend will double in about seven years. (For the math, see the "Rule of 72" in Habit 2: Know and Use Basic Investing Math.) So in seven years you'll be earning 6 percent on your original investment. Not bad, right? Even better is this: If the interest rate environment seven years down the road suggests that 3 percent is still a pretty good yield, and your business is still firing on all cylinders, the share price will go up—up enough to bring that yield back to 3 percent from 6 percent. That implies— you guessed it—that the share price will double. So 6 percent plus a 2X gain in the price of the shares you own . . . not too shabby, right?

I have come to look for something that doesn't get reported as a statistic in any financial portal I've found so far: the consistency and persistency of dividend *raises*. How often has the company raised its dividend? How many times in the past ten years has the company raised its dividend? Some companies proudly proclaim they've raised their dividends for each of the past, say forty-six, years. But this fact doesn't show up anywhere except in the company annual report or website.

Using the *Value Line Investment Survey* (again a testimonial to the excellence of *Value Line*), which shows fifteen years of dividend payment history, I've been tallying the number of dividend *raises* in the past ten years for my core *100 Best Stocks*. The results show above in the far right hand column of Table 22.1.

TIMING, FREQUENCY, ECONOMIC VALUE

The number of dividend increases doesn't necessarily speak to the size or significance of those increases. Companies can raise their dividend from 60 cents to 61 cents, and get credit for a "raise." That's okay, but it doesn't put a whole lot more moolah into the bank account. So I compiled a list of "Dividend Aggressors," published in The *100 Best Stocks to Buy in 2013*. These stocks not only have a track record of steady increases but also have a record of *substantial* increases and, sometimes, a stated policy or goal with respect to raising dividends.

From where I sit, such companies and their management teams are really behaving in the interest of their shareholders.

Swing High, Swing Low

I don't know if this should really be a "habit." But here goes, anyway, if you accept the risk and have the time to dedicate to it.

Stocks go up, and stocks go down. Sometimes there's a darned good reason for that; sometimes stocks just go up and down with the general market. Sometimes, as discussed in the last habit, Habit 21: React, But Don't Overreact, to News, stocks get "hit" with a big institutionally driven crunch after some piece of bad short-term news.

You can make some current cash on this, through what is known as *swing* trading. Swing traders recognize short-term opportunities and overreactions and will move into and out of stocks for a few days or a few weeks to try to capitalize on them.

Now I know this sounds like "market timing," and it is, to a degree. And, as many published research studies have told us, you can't time the markets. Nobody really can. That's true, in general, but how is a Spanish bank failure really going to affect a company such as CarMax that only sells used cars in the United States? When CarMax gets hit for a buck and a half when the Dow is down 200 points because of European turmoil, could you make an argument to buy CarMax? Probably, yes. With some risk, no doubt, but probably, yes.

In Habit 5: Segment, or "Tier," Your Portfolio, I shared three tiers of ownership: (1) *foundation* investments that don't change much and provide steady returns, (2) *rotational* investments that you may choose to move in and out of depending on more global trends, like a strong energy market or a weak financial sector, and (3) *opportunistic* investments that cash in on shorter term opportunities to enhance the total return of the portfolio. These are not specific accounts but rather are specific segments of *thinking* and behavior about your stock portfolio.

If you have a value perspective, that is, an orientation about the long-term value of the businesses you invest in, that makes it easier to spot these opportunities. Does it make sense that, say, Europe-centered oil giant Total S.A. is down a third because of the European slowdown and declining energy prices, while still paying a 6 percent dividend? Maybe, but probably not.

There is no proven formula for doing this, or else everyone would, and these opportunities would cease to exist. And I'm not recommending doing swing trading all the time. But once in a while, it doesn't hurt to get in and stay active—again *if* you have the time and risk appetite for it, and *if* you're only dealing with money you could afford to lose if it doesn't work out. Discipline is key. The willingness to admit that you're wrong and take a loss once in a while is also essential.

Buying and Writing

Way back in Habit 19: Buy Smart—When You Decide to Buy, I introduced the idea of options. Options are derivative securities (scary, yes, but don't be scared away) that allow you to convert time and opportunity into cash. When you have a long-term investment portfolio, you have a lot of opportunity, so why not turn it into some short-term cash in the bank? The strategy here is the simplest, most straightforward, most risk-free use of options: the so-called "buy-write," also known as "selling covered calls." You buy (or own already) some shares, and you *write*, or sell, options against the shares, to collect a *premium*, that is, cash. You can do this over and over, collecting cash over and over, so long as the shares don't rise above the *strike price*, which would trigger a sale of the shares.

Now, I'll repeat my little basic option explanation from Habit 19:

> *Options are market-traded securities designed to allow an investor (or trader) to buy or sell the right to buy or sell a security at a fixed, determined price ("strike price"), by a fixed, predetermined future date ("expiration date"). That right is worth money and thus is bought or sold as a separate security. The price of that option security is known as a premium. The buyer of an option pays the premium; the seller collects it as cash.*

> *There are two types of options. An option to buy a security at a strike price by a certain expiration date is called a call; an option to sell a security at a strike price by a certain date is called a put. An investor who wanted to bet on a stock going up would buy a call, because the call would increase in value as a stock approached and especially as it exceeded the strike price. An investor who wanted to bet on a stock going down would buy a put, giving him the right to sell the stock at a fixed price, which could come in handy if the stock dropped below that fixed price.*

> *So an investor "bullish" on Intel (current price $27.50) might buy September 28 calls (current month May) and pay, say, $1 for them. If the stock is still at $27.50 in September at the expiration date, the*

calls will be worthless, but in May they have a value, because who knows—the stock could go to $32 by September. Investors and traders pay the premium to get this possibility. The seller of the call option, presumably who owns the Intel shares, wants to earn the $1 premium, and hopes the stock closes at $27.99 on the expiration date.

At this point, I introduced a more complex way to make money selling options—*selling puts* to reap current cash while locking in a specific price to buy the stock, which was okay anyway according to your previous analysis.

Now I'll return to the more basic, more understandable premise of selling covered calls. Make yourself be the person selling those Intel calls. You will collect a buck today and give up the *possible*—but not probable—opportunity that the stock will rise to $32. You're trading this opportunity for the bird-in-hand $1 in cash, willing to forgo the $32 "opportunity." It should be mentioned that you still retain the risk of the stock going down.

So you would write the call options, collect the premium, and hope that the stock closes just shy of the strike price at the expiration date. You can do this over and over, choosing a new strike price each time you do it. Typically you can do it for one-month time intervals, but some fast trading stocks actually have weekly option contracts now. You can also go for longer periods, say three months, and collect larger premiums, though at the risk of missing out on greater gains.

You can learn more about this through a variety of sources, including your own brokerage. The "how to sell covered calls" page at Fidelity (*www.fidelity.com/viewpoints/ how-to-sell-covered-calls*) is but one good example.

Like many more complex investing strategies, it pays to practice—you can "paper trade" (hypothetical trades on paper instead of the real thing) until you feel more comfortable with the analysis and mechanics of the trade.

Get Into the Habit

- Look for solid dividend paying stocks to build a current cash return.
- Look for companies with a steady track record of dividend *increases.*
- If you're a more active investor, capitalize on swing trading opportunities when they present themselves.
- Learn how to sell covered calls to produce or enhance current income.

HABIT 23

Don't Marry Your Investments

*"All marriages are happy. It's the living together
afterward that causes all the trouble."*

At least that's the way Canadian playwright Richard Hull looks
at it. Although it probably wasn't meant this way, there's a certain truth to this statement for all investors.

You grind and grind over whether to buy a company. You
finally make up your mind. You watch the prices and look for
a reasonable entry point. You buy it, and now you own it.

You may have been absolutely, positively sure in the beginning. Or there might have been a little trepidation over the
decision. Did you consider everything? Is this business a good
business? One that you can only see a few bits and pieces of
through the numbers, on the street, on the web, from a few
experiences, and so forth? Did you buy it at the right time?
For the right price?

Yes, it is a bit like getting married—at least in the beginning. You may be thrilled to pieces and blind to any signs that
your partner may not, in fact, turn out to be the right one. Or
you might be a little wary in the first place, but willing to commit to whatever is necessary to make it work.

Either way, you've made a big decision. Now what?

Unlike marriages, which imply a "until death do you part" commitment (at least I think it's still this way), a decision to own a stock is not a marriage. It may feel like one in the beginning, but it is not. There is no long-term commitment to the stock. If things don't turn out the way you expected, you can just walk away.

Hallelujah. Stock investing is easier than marriage. But is it really easy for most of us to walk away from a stock?

By our own human nature and competitive spirit, we are all programmed to want to win; to want to come out ahead; to want to beat the odds and appear smart at the next cocktail party. We hate to lose, and we hate to have any kind of relationship go sour. So what do we do? We buy a stock. Then when things start to go sideways, we wait. We wait for them to get better. "Surely I was right, and the market was wrong, don't you think?" That's a phrase that's heard—or thought—over and over again in investing circles.

Like a bad marriage, we tend to hold out hoping things will get better. Hoping that we were right in the first place, and what's happened recently is just an anomaly. Hope beyond hope. It's because that's what we *want* to happen, and probably somewhere or another in our investing past, it *did* happen.

But those of you who have been through a relationship collapse know that neither instant nor permanent recovery is likely. And that's with marriages, where you can do something about it. How about stocks, where you really can't? You can't alter the course of events. Yet, you're still emotionally wrapped up in the price and performance of the stock. That's not a good place to be.

So Habit 23: Don't Marry Your Investments is really about *not* forming a habit. Avoid the habit of marrying your investments. What does that mean? It means you should always buy, hold, and sell rationally, not emotionally. It's a business relationship, not an emotional relationship. It's about winning, but not winning at the expense of losing. It's about not becoming too infatuated in the first place. It's about not becoming attached. And it's about not becoming angry.

Be Impersonal

Marriage is a loving, personal commitment. It is a give-and-take effort to realize happiness for the long term, a happiness that is greater than possible for the two entities if they would live apart. One plus one equals three, but it takes work to get to three.

Such is not the case at all with an investment. You'll put some work into deciding to buy a business, and you'll put at least a little work, as is described by other habits, into *owning* it.

But it is *not* an emotional commitment, not at all. There is nothing to say—nothing contractual, nothing owing to tradition, to ethics, to manners, even to common sense—that you have to own a stock forever, or even through the end of tomorrow (unless it's the weekend and the markets are closed!)

You can hit the off switch any time you want, for any reason. You change your mind about the stock, find something better, or simply want to get conservative for a while, just pound the sell button. You won't get any strange glares from your mother or from your mother-in-law.

Don't let your ego or any other kind of emotional attachment get in the way. Buy when it makes sense to buy. Sell when it's time to sell. And act rationally—don't "look the other way" in the interest of preserving the relationship—because there isn't one.

There Are a Lot of Choices Out There

Unlike a marriage, if someone cuter comes along while you're at lunch, go for it! That is, if you're sure that they're cuter.

Actually, I don't advocate trading back and forth, into and out of stocks, just because something else out there winks at you. If you've done your homework, what you have is probably good enough until clearly demonstrated not to be. And that wink may not be a serious gesture; it may just be more eye-catching than real. And you'll pay a little—probably that $10 brokerage commission, times two (one sale, one purchase)—to make the switch. If your initial investment analysis is any good at all, the original is probably a keeper; it should take more than a wink to make you push the button.

That said, there are thousands of investment possibilities, and if you become a bit sour on the one you have for any reason, you should look for a switch. You can change industries entirely, or even go from a stock to a fund or a bond. Or you can simply switch to another firm in the same business, if you think that company's prospects are a little better or the stock is a little cheaper or the dividend is a little better or some such.

A little bit of commitment to your investments is probably good—it motivates a deeper consideration both of the sale and of the original purchase. But too much fidelity can get you into trouble (my apologies to the large brokerage firm and fund manager headquartered in Boston of that name.)

Don't Throw Good Money after Bad

The need and desire to win can take us to some pretty strange places. Dang—I invested $5,000 in XYZ last week at $50, and now the share price is down to $40! Time to buy more, right?

Well, it might actually be. But that should be considered as a whole 'nother investment decision, not something drawn to support the original investment decision. Investors get so wrapped up with coming out ahead that they insist that their sure bets are—well—sure bets. It's a form of what psychologists call "cognitive dissonance"—a separation from reality in the interest of making two contradictory thoughts or ideas work together. In this instance, those thoughts are, "My stock pick had to be right," and "It fell 20 percent last week." The 20 percent must be wrong, we choose to ignore it; the stock pick must still be right. In essence, "look the other way" on factor number two.

As an investor, you're a businessperson. You act rationally, not emotionally. As such, any time you feel such "cognitive dissonance" coming on, you should do something about it.

Be Willing to Accept Failure

There may be no more important piece of advice to an investor than this: You aren't always going to win; nobody does, so the quicker you accept failure and move on, the better. That's certainly true with investments, and it's probably true with marriages—at least the bad ones—too.

Which relates to . . .

Don't Get Mad (or Get Even)

Again, investors get emotionally attached, and when you're emotionally attached and something doesn't go your way, you may tend to get angry. "That stupid market . . ."

And then you "get even" by doubling down on the now-cheaper stock.

I'll admit, at the risk of sounding a little sexist, that this is more of a male tendency. I'm not sure if this has been studied—it probably has—but it is certainly my experience. Guys want to win even more than gals; gals tend to be a little thicker-skinned about this. They cut their losses and move on to something else. Women just seem to take blows to their ego better. That's good—and I know some studies have pointed to better investing performance from women who are willing to take risks. Maybe it's because they don't get mad when they lose.

Regardless, that's them, and this book is about you. Don't get emotionally attached, don't get mad, and don't try to get even. You won't succeed.

Get Into the Habit

- Do not become emotionally attached to your investments.
- Do not become emotionally attached to your investments.
- Do not become emotionally attached to your investments.

HABIT 24

Sell When There's Something Better to Buy

If it's hard to figure out when to buy a stock, it's even harder to figure out when to sell. As I described in Habit 23, people tend to "get married" to their investment decisions, feeling somehow that if it isn't right, maybe time will help, and things will get better. Or they're just too arrogant to admit that they made a mistake. There are lots of reasons why people hold on to investments for too long a time.

I will counter this notion with a piece of common wisdom: *hope is not a strategy.*

So when *do* you sell? Is there ever a perfectly "right" time? If a stock is trending downward, is there a fixed time or percentage loss point at which you should cut your losses? When a stock is trending upward, should you harvest the gains at some point?

Here's the fundamental truth: buying and selling should be much the same process. Let's look at it from the point of view of selling. When should you sell? Simply, *when there's something else better to buy.* Something else better for future returns, something else better for safety, something else better for

timeliness or synchronization with overall business trends—
something else better for *any* reason. That something else
can be another stock, a futures contract, or even a house or a
home improvement if that's the best place to put your money.
It can also be cash—sell that stock when . . . when what? When
cash is a better investment. Or when you need the money,
which is another way of saying that cash is a better investment.

A sell decision, like all investing decisions, at the end of
the day is about the best deployment of *your* capital. If company XYZ is no longer the best place for you to deploy your
hard-earned capital, why hang onto it? That decision can be
triggered by a long, slow change of events or the business climate around the company. Or it can be triggered by a sudden
news event—although I cautioned in Habit 21 that a one-timer
news event often doesn't change the long-term prospects of a
business very much.

Sell decisions, like buy decisions, are about doing your
homework. They're about using a rational approach to make
a rational decision. If this is done right, no sell decision will
be taken too soon, and no sell decision will be taken too late.
Of course you won't know everything, so it's doubtful that
you'll always sell at the all-time high price of a stock. But if you
deploy this discipline, you'll almost certainly come out ahead.

It may seem self explanatory upon closer observation,
but—at the risk of repeating—the time to sell is simple: sell
when there's something better to buy.

Even Cash Can Be Something Better to Buy

When you think of how to deploy the "sell when there's something better to buy" wisdom, you usually think of switching
from one stock to another. You think about selling company
XYZ to buy company ABC, either a stronger competitor or a
company in another, more promising industry.

This isn't wrong. It just isn't the complete story.

I suggested it in the opening part of this habit but will emphasize it again: Cash is a valid choice to consider as an investment alternative. Of course, cash as an investment comes in several forms—bank CDs, money market funds, and so forth. That's almost beside the point, but you should be familiar with those alternatives and their current yields.

The real point is that cash represents capital, and sometimes that capital is just plain best left on the sidelines to wait for the best opportunity, to weather a storm, or to strengthen your own personal financial situation and make it more flexible. Any of these are good reasons. If cash is a better place for your capital than company XYZ, hit the sell button.

DON'T WHIFF BECAUSE OF TAXES

It happens all the time. The smartest investors come up with the smartest sell moves, then swing and miss when they finally go for the trading screen on their broker's website. They just don't do it. Why? Because they're worried about paying taxes on the gains.

In my experience, for all but a few sell decisions, this can get you into trouble. You whiff on the sale that otherwise made sense, then things change for the worse. There are some occasions, such as a year where you have a large windfall gain or income from something else, where it might make sense to defer the stock sale for a short time to put it into a different tax year. But you should decide this consciously, in contact with a tax advisor if need be—and it should be the exception, not the rule.

Selling with Limits—A Good Idea?

A lot of brokers and advisers recommend using so-called limit orders, or fixed-price orders, to force more disciplined sales, particularly when you don't have time to watch a stock during the day or during a given period of time.

A limit order is an order placed for a configurable duration of time to buy or sell a stock at a predetermined price. The time duration choices are usually "day only," meaning for the duration of the trading day the order is placed, or "good till cancelled," meaning the order remains in place until cancelled or executed.

Limit sell orders are usually placed to capture a gain on the upside if the stock rises to that price level. Suppose you own Intel, and the current price is $26.75. You could place a limit order to "sell, day only, at 27" (this is usually accomplished with data entry on a broker's website, not by typing out a sentence). You go off to work, while an "offer" is placed in the market at a fixed price of 27, meaning that you're offering your shares to any buyer at that price. If the price hits 27, your shares will sell, assuming there are enough buyers in the market to absorb *all* the shares offered at that price. (You can see the potential wisdom of placing your limit at $26.99 to sell before the likely larger number of offers at the round number of 27.)

Advisers will suggest you place a limit perhaps 10 percent ahead of the current stock price, in this case, perhaps at $30.50 or thereabouts, "good till cancelled." It becomes a sell *target*. If the stock gains 10 percent, you'll harvest the 10 percent gain, more or less automatically. That's good for discipline; that's also good for ensuring a real cash gain from your investment.

But the question to ask yourself—and this is usually left out by the advisers who suggest this—is: "At a price of $30.50, is Intel still the best place for me to deploy my capital? Is it the best investment? Is there something else better to buy?

If the answer is yes, go ahead and set up the limit order. If the answer is no, then don't do it, and don't be talked into it.

A much more common ploy suggested by brokers and advisers is the so-called *stop-loss* order. A "stop" order is similar to a limit order, except that instead of representing an actual fixed price bid or offer in the marketplace, it sits in the background and only becomes an active *market* order when triggered by a certain price. That means that when the price trigger is reached, an active market order will launch, and the trade will happen at whatever the current market will bear.

So you buy 100 shares of Intel at $27.75 and decide that if it drops 10 percent (the common wisdom usually suggested by advisers and a broad swath of investment media) you want to cut your losses and sell. So you might set up a stop loss order, good till cancelled, at $25. What happens? Nothing, until the stock drops to $25. When any trade executes at $25 *or below*, your order becomes an active market order. So if Intel serves up some bad earnings news and opens the day at $24, do you get $25 for your shares? Nope—you get $24 or whatever the market will bear at the instant your order becomes active.

Stop-loss orders, like their limit upside counterpart, are designed as a "safety net" and to make sure you don't get buried deeper in a tumbling stock. Again, for the sake of discipline, that's not always a bad idea, particularly if you're too occupied with other things to watch it closely. But there are two things to consider. First, the markets are very good at sniffing out stop loss orders, especially at nice round numbers like $25. Professional traders and market makers (dealers) can play tricks to knock the price down to trigger the stop, only to scoop up shares at a bargain price for their own gain. (After watching the markets for a long time, you'll come to note how many daily "lows" are at "$25" or "$24.95" or some other round number.)

But the real bugaboo—and you probably guessed by now—is that no decision has been made about whether Intel at $25 is the best place for your capital. At $25, is there something else better to buy? You could argue "cash" when a stock gouges you like this. That suggests that maybe something was wrong with your analysis, and the safer bet is to "go cash" until you have enough time to reappraise. That's fine, but it needs to be a conscious decision.

Sell when there's something else better to buy. Know what you're doing. Don't just sell at 10 percent without any rationale. That's for people who don't know what they're doing.

Not Sure? Try Selling Half

Okay, you've read through twenty-three and one half habits, and you still don't trust yourself to recognize the best times to buy or the best time to sell.

Join the crowd.

There is, and always will be, a lot of uncertainty in investing. There has to be. If investments all behaved in predictable, consistent ways, we'd all make the same buy decisions and the same sell decisions. It would be too easy. Trouble is, if we made all the same decisions at the same time, there wouldn't be a buyer in the market when you came to sell, and there wouldn't be a seller in the market when you came to buy! These "counterparties" would all be trying to do the same thing—not the opposing thing—that you're trying to do!

That uncertainty makes the markets work. It also makes it hard for you to make an absolute decision about whether to buy or sell a stock. This is perfectly understandable; it is the nature of the game.

So you think you want to sell? You have in mind something else better to buy (even cash). The assumptions about your investment may have changed, but you're not completely sure. What do you do?

In my experience, I've found that so-called "half selling" makes a lot of sense. Sell half of your holding, reaping some cash or capital for another investment, and keep the other half "on the table" in case you were right about the company in the first place. By half selling, you reduce your risk in that company, but still participate if things turn out.

You can also "quarter sell" or sell some other fraction if you're feeling more or less tentative, and have enough shares to have such a division make sense. By half selling (or half buying), you preserve some capital (or part of your investment) for another action later, hopefully at a better price.

Either way, the "half" approach will help you sleep better at night. You'll feel better because you took action and made a move towards safety or another investment, but you'll also feel better if your original analysis turns out to be right.

Get Into the Habit

- Only sell if there's something better to buy.
- Remember—cash can be "something better to buy."
- Use limits only within the sell-when-there's-something-better-to-buy principle, not for their own sake or for a stab-in-the-dark price level.
- If you aren't sure, try selling half.

HABIT 25

Measure Your Results

"What can be measured can be understood;
what can be understood can be altered."

So goes the wisdom-laden quote from fantasy-science fiction author Katherine Neville from her fascinating book *The Eight.* Such a statement by itself may make fascinating reading, but more to the point, it makes for a hugely important philosophical guidepost for investing. Heck, for all of your personal finances, for that matter. Even for your career and your life.

It's funny how humans measure some things to the nearest grain, like the price of gas or a gallon of milk, and let other things in their life run their own course with only infrequent stops, if any stops at all. Is it a matter of trust? Are you *so* good with personal finance and investing that you can *assume* that everything will come out right?

Or is it "ignorance is bliss?" "What I don't know can't hurt me." Or "Well, I can't do anything about it anyway." Or "I'm doing terribly, and I just can't bear to look." All of these, as I've discovered (and experienced personally over the years) are simple outcomes of human nature.

I think you can kind of see where this is going. Habit 25: Measure Your Results is a simple and short one, appropriately saved for last. You should check your investments at least annually to see how you're performing. How you did, and how you're doing. Really better is to review once a quarter, even once a month. The world changes fast.

Don't hide your head in the sand.

The Regular Review

If you work in an organization, you get a regular review. It goes a bit like the "SWOT" analysis rolled out in Habit 13: Put on Your Marketing Hat. Your boss will review your strengths, your weaknesses, your opportunities, and your threats. If it's an adequately done review, you'll know where you stand and what to do going forward.

Your investment review should produce a similar result, with perhaps a little more detail.

Take a look at your holdings. Check them against (1) where you bought them, and (2) where they were at the last review. Most likely, some are doing well compared to your assumptions; some are not. Go through each investment and test it to see if it still belongs. It's like doing the buy-sell analysis all over again, but unless it has vastly deviated from your expectations, you probably don't have to do too much detail.

Do a SWOT analysis for each investment, and a review of the three pros, three cons (from Habit 17: Do Your Threes—Three Pros, Three Cons) is a good idea too. Make sure your picks are still your picks, and be prepared to make changes.

From there, you might do a SWOT analysis on your whole portfolio. You may decide that it's time to make adjustments. You may decide that it's *not*. Choosing to do nothing is a perfectly good decision—if it's made consciously and rationally.

IT'S NOT JUST A TAXING MATTER

Some people review their investments only once a year—at tax time! Because they have to—they have to prepare a Schedule D Statement of Capital Gains and Losses. This is probably *not* the time to do such a review. Your mind will be on other things.

Learn From Your Mistakes

It is said that all education is based upon learning from our mistakes and learning from the mistakes of others. As an obvious fallout from this idea, you should analyze your investments—*all* investments, those on which you gain and those on which you lose—to decipher what you did right and what you did wrong.

When something works or doesn't work, do an honest assessment of why or why not. Sometimes it helps to write it down, so you can "jell" the thought and refer back to it later and learn more surely how not to repeat the mistake. Call it your "investment diary" if you'd like.

Either way measure, understand, and alter when necessary.

Only then will you gain what you should from the experience, and become a better investor.

Get Into the Habit

- Do a regular performance review of your investments, at least annually, but quarterly or monthly may make more sense, depending on how "active" your investments are.
- Make a brief "buy-sell" determination for each investment. Do SWOT, and do three pros and three cons.
- Keep a diary of your successes and failures.
- Learn from your mistakes.
- *Now* go make a million bucks.

The 25 Habits at a Glance

PART I

Style for Success:
Crafting Your Individual Investing Style

Habit 1: Know Yourself—and Know What to Expect

- Know what you're trying to accomplish. Say it out loud, discuss it with your family, and write it down.
- Know what's realistic to expect.
- Decide if you are happy meeting, exceeding, or staying slightly under market returns, given the risk and energy involved.
- Invest what you can afford to lose.
- Make sure everyone in your family is on board.

Habit 2: Know and Use Basic Investing Math

- Always remember the power of compounding.
- Strive to make "just a few dollars more."
- Know the true cost of professional management and fund fees.
- Practice your "Rule of 72" shorthand. It comes in handy, and you can impress your friends too!
- Think in terms of compounded rates of return—it's more conservative and more realistic.

Habit 3: Get the Right—and Right Amount of—Information

- Decide how much time you have, and want to spend, staying informed.
- Think about what you need or want among the five categories: Economic Trends, Industry Trends, Financial Stuff, Soft Stuff, and Analysis.
- Review sources in each category and select based on their value.
- Review your choices occasionally; drop the ones that aren't adding much; try others on for size.
- Tap into informal networks—friends, family, and industry insiders.
- Share information sources with other investors or friends, to cut cost or leverage each other's time.

Habit 4: Find Your Diversification Sweet Spot

- Realize the myths and costs of diversification.
- Avoid overlapping funds and other forms of overdiversification.
- Diversify "deeper" than simple asset allocation. Realize that the mix of stocks versus bonds versus cash versus other doesn't go far enough without knowing what's beneath the surface.
- Diversify across multiple "smart" dimensions—industry, risk profile, time horizon and funds vs. individual company stocks.
- Set yourself up to choose and manage between five and ten companies as your primary "focus" investments.

Habit 5: Segment, or "Tier," Your Portfolio

- Divide your investments into tiers—either by specifically segmenting accounts or dividing simply in your mind (a written list will help you keep track).
- Decide how much of your portfolio should be in each tier, and set expectations for each tier.

- Spend more time managing the more active tiers—the most time devoted to the Opportunistic portfolio, the less to the Rotational, then the least to the Foundation portfolio.
- When considering a new investment, think about what tier it should reside in.
- Shop for the best investments for each tier.

Habit 6: Work Hard *and* Work Smart

- Do the homework, just as if you're buying and owning the whole business.
- Set aside the time to do it right, both initially and ongoing.
- Get help where you need it—in the form of professional advisers and in the form of fund investments.
- Turn it into a routine.

PART II

Appraise for Success: Finding Your Very Best Investments

Habit 7: Buy Like You're Buying a Business

- Think of buying a stock like you're buying 100 percent of the business.
- Always think about the business, *and then* look at the price.
- Don't fall for something just because it sounds like a good idea.

Habit 8: Buy What You Understand, Understand What You Buy

- Make sure you understand a company you're thinking about owning.

- Be able to state the company's business in a few simple statements to—say—a family member.
- Make sure you have the background and the connections to find out what you need to know about a company.
- If you don't understand it, don't buy it. Move on. There are plenty of companies out there.

Habit 9: Appraise Funds Realistically

- Understand the advantages of funds vs. individual stocks, know where funds may better meet your needs, and act accordingly. Map out a *strategy* for using funds in your portfolio—e.g., to achieve international diversification, exposure to commodities, exposure to small-cap stocks, etc.
- Know how traditional mutual funds and ETFs compare; be prepared to shop the assortment of mutual funds and ETFs to fill the gaps in your portfolio.
- Evaluate funds by objective congruence, holdings, performance, and cost. Test the fund to see if it really does what it says it does, and what *you* want it to do.
- Avoid buying overlapping funds—too much diversification.
- Don't assume that just because the fund comes from a famous Wall Street firm and is wrapped up in a nice package, that it is right for you. It is like any other product and should be evaluated accordingly.

Habit 10: Value Thy Fundamentals

- Remember that fundamentals are the scorecard of the past, while intangibles such as brand and marketplace, and management excellence foretell the scorecard of the future.
- Keep in mind that fundamentals measure absolute business performance, relative performance over time (trends), and efficiency.

- Use fundamentals as a measure of (1) how strong a company is in the marketplace and (2) how effectively management converts that strength into profits.
- Develop your own list of "strategic fundamentals" (starting with the one provided, if you want). Use that list as an "acid test" for companies you own or evaluate to buy.

Habit 11: Look for Cash in All the Right Places

- Make the Statement of Cash Flows part of your normal review process.
- Determine whether the company is producing or consuming cash (capital).
- Determine if cash flows are well managed and in control.
- Check to see that the company is returning cash to investors on a regular basis.

Habit 12: Don't Forget the Intangibles

- Recognize and realize that intangibles are about the future, while financials are about the past.
- Look for "moats"—sustainable competitive advantages.
- Examine, one by one, the following (some may be more elusive than others):
    1. Brand
    2. Market leadership and position
    3. Customer loyalty
    4. Innovation excellence
    5. Channel excellence
    6. Supply chain excellence
    7. Management excellence

- Absorb intangible information by regularly reading about the company in the news, visits to the company and/or its websites, and listening to what others—personal or professional—have to say about the company.

Habit 13: Put on Your Marketing Hat

- Think about companies you own—or want to buy—as a marketer would.
- Decide where the company positions itself (Walmart–Target–Nordstrom as an example), and decide whether the company is succeeding with this positioning.
- Look for solid niche players and signs of niche leadership.
- Look at a company's product portfolio—and the company itself—to seek out Stars and Cash Cows.
- Determine if the company is gaining share—and share (mindshare) of customer.
- Decide whether the company presents itself clearly and effectively in the marketplace. Does it convey value to its customers?
- Identify three strengths, weaknesses, opportunities, and threats for each company. Decide if any of the weaknesses or threats are showstoppers.

Habit 14: Put on Your Street Shoes

- Spend at least a little time, preferably each week, checking out businesses you own or might want to invest in. Do it locally, when you travel, and through friends, family, and acquaintances.
- Pay attention to your own interactions, purchases, and experiences with a company. Could it have been better? Does someone else do it better?
- Look at the level of customer activity, appearance of facilities, and the attitude and helpfulness of employees.
- Check out websites. Give a "plus" to companies with clear, accessible, helpful messages about their products and how they benefit *you*.
- Watch the ads. Are they effective? What are they really telling you?

- Get into the "buzz" network through friends, employers, employees of other companies, and through financial, industry, and trade media.

Habit 15: Sense the Management Style

- Realize from the beginning that understanding management and leadership effectiveness is a "read between the lines" exercise.
- Look for signs of achievement, not signs of power. As Bill Clinton once said, "power by example, not examples of power."
- Look for signs of customer focus, solid and rational vision, winning culture, winning products, clear, crisp, useful messages, and a solid reputation and management "brand."
- Again remember—you're acquiring a sense. If you think you'd like to work for the company, you're on the right track.

Habit 16: Look for Signs of Value, Signs of Unvalue

- Create a checklist (or use the one described in Habit 16).
- Check it twice.
- Find out who is naughty or nice.
- If Santa never comes, consider adjusting the checklist.

Habit 17: Do Your Threes—Three Pros, Three Cons

- Think in terms of threes—three strengths, three weaknesses, or three pros and three cons.
- Write them down, especially for the "final analysis" of a company.
- Amend and adjust as necessary.
- Try it. You'll like it. It works.

Habit 18: Buy with a Margin of Safety

- Look at a business value as the sum of *all* future cash flows.
- Look at the ratios. Use them as a guide to future returns and to compare alternatives.
- Pretend you're buying the whole business—*still* want to buy it?
- Give yourself an extra margin of safety, by buying at a price dip, just in case.

PART III

Own for Success: Getting the Most Out of Your Portfolio

Habit 19: Buy Smart—When You Decide to Buy

- Be patient. Watch the stock for a few days at least before jumping in.
- Buy when you decide to buy; use market orders; don't play games to try to save a few cents.
- Add to your investments regularly; take advantage of dollar cost averaging.
- If so inclined, sell *put* options to earn a little more from your buying decisions.

Habit 20: Keep Your Finger on the Pulse

- Make regular time to scan the news, get quotes, and check the progress of companies you own.
- Observe quarterly financial reports carefully and listen to the conference calls.

- Put your street shoes on. Wander around, sense the business, sense the customers, and make sure the business is still on track.
- Keep tabs on the competition.
- Keep in touch with industry experts.

Habit 21: React, But Don't Overreact, to News

- Stop, look, and listen to new news announcements. Don't ignore them.
- React by digging further.
- Think of yourself as the owner.
- Don't overreact with an ill-considered sell (or buy) reflex.

Habit 22: Pay Yourself

- Look for solid dividend paying stocks to build a current cash return.
- Look for companies with a steady track record of dividend *increases*.
- If you're a more active investor, capitalize on swing trading opportunities when they present themselves.
- Learn how to sell covered calls to produce or enhance current income.

Habit 23: Don't Marry Your Investments

- Do not become emotionally attached to your investments.
- Do not become emotionally attached to your investments.
- Do not become emotionally attached to your investments.

Habit 24: Sell When There's Something Better to Buy

- Only sell if there's something better to buy.
- Remember—cash can be "something better to buy."
- Use limits only within the sell-when-there's-something-better-to-buy principle, not for their own sake or for a stab-in-the-dark price level.
- If you aren't sure, try selling half.

Habit 25: Measure Your Results

- Keep a diary of your successes and failures.
- Learn from your mistakes.
- *Now* go make a million bucks.

INDEX

About the Author

Peter Sander (Granite Bay, CA) is an author, researcher, and consultant in the fields of personal finance, business, and location reference. He has written thirty-five books, including *Value Investing for Dummies*, *The 100 Best Exchange-Traded Funds You Can Buy 2012*, *What Would Steve Jobs Do?*, *101 Things Everyone Should Know about Economics*, and *Cities Ranked & Rated*. He is also the author of numerous articles and columns on investment strategies. He has an MBA from Indiana University and has completed Certified Financial Planner (CFP) education and examination requirements.